ALEXANDRA PENNEY

Great Sex

G. P. PUTNAM'S SONS
NEW YORK

G. P. Putnam's Sons
PUBLISHERS SINCE 1838
200 Madison Avenue
New York, NY 10016

Library of Congress Cataloging in Publication Data

Penney, Alexandra.
    Great sex.

    1. Sex. I. Title.
HQ16.P46 1985   613.9'6   84-24804
ISBN 0-399-13031-4

Printed in the United States of America

1 2 3 4 5 6 7 8 9 10

For J. B. P.

Contents

1 September, New York   11
2 What's Great Sex?   24
3 Who's Sexy Now?   29
4 September, Italy   34
5 How to Beat Sexual Gridlock   42
6 P.A.—What No One Likes to Talk About   51
7 The Hottest Spots   59
8 September, Italy, continued   74
9 Hands On   80

10 *The Point of No Return*   *86*

11 *Ultimate Sex*   *93*

12 *Taboo and Terrific*   *108*

13 *October*   *122*

14 *Erection-Wreckers*   *131*

15 *Can We Talk?*   *140*

16 *The Great Frequency Debate*
     (HOW OFTEN IS EVERYONE ELSE DOING IT
     —AND WHAT IF YOU'RE NOT DOING IT
     AT ALL?)   *158*

17 *Four Months Later*   *166*

18 *The New Frontier*   *172*

19 *The Night of Endless Pleasure*   *185*

20 *Love-Drugs*   *198*

21 *Secrets of a Truly Seductive Woman*   *202*

ACKNOWLEDGMENTS

To my long-suffering and patient Norman who soothed and loved me all the way through . . .

I could never have written this book without the help and encouragement of Phyllis Grann, a very special editor and publisher, John Hawkins, ne-plus-ultra-and-always-there-agent, and Howard Kaminsky who unstintingly gave his friendship, time, wit, and wonderful ideas.

Grateful thanks go to Myrna Blyth who always

called at the right moment, Edward Caracci, Margot Cohn, Corcil, Dawn of the Cupping Room Cafe, Frank Donnelly, Hester Diamond and Ralph Kaminsky, Madeline Frisk Fleishman, Peter Fleishman, the elusive and delightful Tuna B. Fish, Barry Gingell, Jeanna Gollobin, Jim Henderson, Asher Jason, Susan Kaminsky, Robert Levine, Suzanne Levine, Harriet Love who sent up encouragement and the parcels, Ivo Lupis, Phyllis Posnick, Betsey Roberts, Stone Roberts, Mary Ann Spencer, Suga, Larry Totah. And to the California contingent: Martin Berman, executive producer of *Hour Magazine* and Margie Friedman and Ramey Warren who work with him. Also to Room #189 of the Beverly Hills Hotel for its unique contribution to this book. And many thanks to the hotel staff, especially Bill Bigsby and Ron Schaeg.

A special thank-you to my indefatigable researcher Robert Lang, the film scholar and sleuth, who gave valuable suggestions and located the most esoteric material that I needed.

Lastly, not one single page of this book could have happened without Alice Fried Martell, Michael Martell, E.B.S. and Dr. H. R.—I'm immeasurably grateful to you.

Great Sex

CHAPTER 1

September, New York

"YOU'VE GOT TO HELP US entertain these people. It's for Jim's business. They're clients," coaxed Alice, Diana Teague's dearest friend, when she called to invite her to a last-minute dinner. "Okay, okay—I admit it's a major possibility that you'll die of boredom, but *please* come. We need an attractive, dynamic woman like you."

Laughing at Alice's exaggerations, Diana said, "Of course I'll be there if it's so important to you."

"It is. I know you're trying to pack for your trip, but I wouldn't ask you unless we *really* needed you. Come at eight—you can leave early."

Diana hung up the phone, looked at her watch and then at the yellow pad on her desk that listed all the things she had to get done before she left for Paris on Friday.

She was going on vacation. She needed something to shake up her life, to give it some new energy and excitement, so she'd decided to take her two weeks' holiday in Europe, going first to Paris for three days and then heading south to Italy.

She'd been abroad once before, right after college seven years ago, and she had been wanting to go back ever since. She had no specific plans in mind except seeing beautiful sights, and, hopefully, having some "interesting experiences," as she'd said to Alice when she had finally made up her mind to go alone. Sure, she'd love to meet a man—but that was not her goal. She simply wanted some excitement in her life and she was certain she could find that on her own.

She took in a deep breath and looked out at the glinting gray river that wrapped around the east side of Manhattan like a broad steel ribbon. *How* was she ever going to get everything done by Friday? She sorted the folders into three tidy piles: somehow, she assured herself, everything would be taken care of. That's why she was the youngest assistant vice-president in the personnel department of a large New York bank: she got things done.

It was eight thirty before she actually arrived outside the Hartmanns' apartment.

"Diana! I'm so glad you're here! This is turning out to be crazy," Alice told her in the hallway. "We have *six* more guests than we expected! Please just talk to everybody—I have to get things organized in the kitchen."

Diana walked into the living room and, as Jim handed her a drink, she immediately noticed a tall man standing a few feet away from her. Who wouldn't have noticed him? He was handsome in the way a movie star is: Technicolor-blue eyes, waving sunbleached hair, straight nose, classic movie-star chin. He was headed toward the kitchen, and she noticed that he moved with an easy athletic assurance. He's almost *too* good-looking, she thought. What was it that her mother had once said about people from Southern California? Blond, beautiful, and empty-headed.

Her mother would have been dead wrong. Thanks to some nimble last-minute maneuvering on Alice's part, he was seated next to Diana during dinner. She soon learned that his name was Michael Boeting and that he was a well-known architect. Readily ignoring the guest on her left, she sat entranced while he explained that he had indeed come from Los Angeles, moved to New York four months ago, and was leaving for Paris in two days on business. He'd been invited to Alice and Jim's party by a friend who happened to be a new client of Jim's.

They talked nonstop through Alice's marvelous pasta primavera, through the chocolate-pecan pie. They were still talking over coffee in the living room when he abruptly asked:

"Do you mind if I say something personal?"

"Not at all," she replied, feeling a dart of anxiety.

"I don't know if you're involved with anyone" he said, his eyes turning to sapphire in the muted light, "but I want very much to make love to you."

She was so taken aback by his words that she didn't know what to say.

"I usually don't come on this strong," he continued, never taking his eyes off hers, "but I'll be in Paris on Thursday. You'll be there Friday. Why don't you meet me for the weekend?"

"Okay," she heard herself say, as if from a great distance. "I think I'd love it," she added, trying to sound as if this sort of thing happened to her all the time. Could he see through her skin and watch her heart knocking against her ribs? Keep cool, she said to herself, just keep things very cool.

A few minutes later he left the party with the very attractive dark-haired woman who had invited him as her guest.

He called Diana the next day at her office to make arrangements for their meeting.

But as it turned out the plans were unnecessary; when she cleared customs in Paris he was suddenly there.

"I can't believe it's you!" Diana said as he lifted her off her feet in a hug.

"It's no fun coming into an airport alone," he said, carefully setting her down. "I worked late last night, so today's meeting wasn't necessary. Come—"

He took her arm, hailed a porter, and found a taxi: she loved the way he took charge so effortlessly. They settled back—the blue-gray upholstered seats were spotless, not like New York cabs with all that black tape patching up the Naugahyde—and he kissed her softly on the lips. "I'm so excited that you're here. Look! Isn't it beautiful?"

It was early morning in Paris and the sky was streaked with delicate mauves and pinks. The driver negotiated a maze of streets on the Left Bank, then stopped abruptly in front of a small hotel.

The gray-coated clerk, standing behind a reception desk, whose rich wood gleamed with years of rubbing and polishing, looked at them suspiciously through silver-rimmed glasses. Michael handed over her passport and asked that her bags be brought to the room as soon as possible.

They entered one of those small cages that the French call elevators and ascended slowly to the third floor. Diana's heart was literally pounding against her ribs. Michael gave no sign that anything exceptional was about to happen. For the thousandth time since Alice and Jim's party she wondered, *How does he feel about all this?*

The largest tulips in the world were in a tall glass cylinder on the mantel of the fireplace. She had never seen flowers that color—a dark, rich, glorious pink, like the inside of an exotic shell, like a woman's secret lips that have deepened with sexual arousal. The spacious room was decorated in subtle grays: the walls; the deep, soft carpet; the draperies; the heavy bedspread; the dove-gray blotter on the elegant fruitwood writing table.

"Sit in that chair," he commanded. "I have something for you."

He took out a small square package, wrapped in a heavy ivory paper with a crimson cord tied around it. Inside lay a small crystal flaçon. He gently took the bottle from her, twisted the stopper open, and slowly dabbed a delicate, exotic fragrance on her neck, behind her ears, in the crook of her elbows. With every touch her nipples pulled and hardened under her sweater; the warm cashmere felt like hands all over her body.

"Oh, Michael, you're—"

"And this is for you too," he interrupted, still smiling, handing her another beautifully wrapped package.

"Chocolate truffles! How do you know I *adore* them?"

"I knew," he said mysteriously, the intense blue eyes again turning magically to sapphire.

"Now I think you ought to get some rest," he said.

"But I just got here," she protested. Every nerve was awake, every one of her senses was dilated for pleasure.

"No, you should take a nap to get over the jet-lag— and then we'll have a wonderful time."

"No, do let me stay up," she insisted with an especially charming smile. She wanted him so badly that she could feel the warm wetness gathering between her legs.

"A nap is best right now," he said, returning her smile with a disarming one of his own.

She took off her clothes in the bathroom. What she really wanted to do was to go back into the bedroom stark naked and see his reaction, but no, this was his scenario and she'd play it his way—this time.

She reached for her bag just outside the bathroom door in the alcove dressing area and dug out her robe, a pale jade kimono. The light silk on her skin made her feel as fragile and feminine as a camellia.

He had pulled the covers back for her. She slid into the cool luxury of the linen sheets, letting the kimono fall open. Surely he would take off his clothes and get into bed with her now, she thought.

But he did not.

She was saturated with excitement, too aroused to rest, but obediently she closed her eyes. Somehow she drifted off to a dreamless sleep. When she woke, he was sitting in a deep wing-chair, his face half-hidden, a folder of typewritten sheets balanced on his lap. She stretched her body like a tawny cat, feeling salty/sweet wetness lapping between her legs.

"I can't sleep anymore," she declared. "I feel terrific!"

She knew he wanted her: she could see the charged

maleness in his eyes when he had turned his head to watch her body shifting under the light covers.

He rose from the chair and with that loose, easy stride he had, headed for the bathroom.

Now, she thought, now he would come out and take her.

Instead, she heard water running.

Two minutes later, still fully dressed, he came over to the bed with an immaculate white towel. Suspended between a flickering fear of seeming too aggressive and the desire to show him that she too could take the lead, she hesitated, then reached her arms up to pull him down to her.

"Oh, not yet," he said, his blue eyes twinkling. He gently tugged her into a sitting position, slowly and deliberately lifted her arms out of the kimono, and wrapped her in the towel. A jolt of sexual electricity shot through her whole body. He took her by the hand and led her to a steaming bath.

And then he simply turned and walked out of the room.

That bath was an exquisite erotic torture that she would never forget. Slowly she lathered her breasts with the finely milled French soap, watching her nipples turning dark and pointed. Slowly she rolled a soft washcloth between her legs and felt with her fingers for the tiny bud: it was smooth and hard. Her whole body was so sensitized, so open and ready, that she *willed* him to rush through the door and take her—but she could see him sitting back in his chair, calmly reading his papers.

She stayed in the tub, running more hot water until the room turned moist and tropically languorous. When she could stand it no longer, she finally stepped out, her body radiating heat and shining with excitement. She was lightheaded and slightly dizzy from not eating, and the steaming bath had enveloped her in a fever of sensuality.

Someone knocked on the outside door. Michael stood up, placed the folders on the writing table, closed the door to the bathroom so that she couldn't see, and went to answer. Slowly, luxuriously, she began to rub herself with the thick towels, burningly aware of every inch of her body.

There was another knock, this time on the bathroom door. She wrapped herself in a towel and said, "Come in," in a voice she hoped hovered between nonchalant and seductive.

In his hand was a fluted glass filled with champagne. He didn't offer her any but took a long draft and then came over and, bending his head to meet hers, kissed her. As his lips opened she felt clean icy champagne pour from his mouth into hers. Her whole body stiffened. He placed the glass on a small, marble-topped cabinet, slowly unwrapped the towel, let it fall on the gleaming white tile. He took her in his arms and started kissing her, slow, searching kisses, deep inside her mouth. He held her hard against his body.

Suddenly he swooped her up bride-over-the-threshold style and put her on the bed. Looking down at her he began, slowly, torturously slowly, to take off his clothes.

For endless hours there was only that shimmering, silvery room, the bending, curving tulips, the wide bed with the white linen sheets. Only the two of them existed. Nothing else mattered, only his magnificent, supple, muscular body and her open, yielding one, a tangle of hair and skin, an infinitely deep well of wetness and warmth . . .

And then it was seven, the moment when that extraordinary opaline light of Paris is just fading. They left the sheets tossed back, dressed without showering, savoring the deep musky salt-scents of their bodies and walked and walked the quays as the evening darkened.

"Shall we try that restaurant I told you about?" asked Michael, looking down at her, his hair tousled by the light breeze from the Seine. "Or would you prefer room service?" Not waiting for an answer, he put his arms around her, pressing his hands down on the small of her back so that she could feel his hardness. They hastened back to the hotel as Paris wrapped them in her warm, liquid night.

To be continued . . .

A recent report in *Psychology Today* pointed out that of 450 men and women, three-quarters of them said that

hugging,
　kissing,
　　mutual respect,
　　　listening to music,
　　　　eating Haagen-Dazs ice cream,
　　　　Godiva chocolates,
　　　　　accumulating money,
　　　　　　were
　　　　　　better than sex!

Survey after survey confirmed this depressing news: a sizable number of men and women didn't think sex was that big a deal anymore. The *New York Times* bannered a "New Conservatism" in sex, and a *Time* magazine cover story unearthed a "glacial shift" in ways that Americans felt about sexual matters. The cool, casual, let's-rack-up-the-numbers kind of sex that was the big bang of the seventies had led to nothing more than loneliness, emptiness—and probably herpes.

A postmodern phenomenon, Lack of Sexual Desire, has recently begun to make headlines in sex-research journals. Droves of men and women are seeking therapeutic help to deal with the increasingly widespread sexual malaise of the mid-eighties. "Sex therapy clinics," say the directors of the Yale Human Sexuality Program (in an interview in *GQ* magazine, August 1984), "are full of people with inhibited sexual desire—i.e., they are bored with sex. Among the single and divorced men we see the complaint is simply 'Sex isn't what it used to be. It's not that I *can't*. I'm just not very interested.'"

What in the world has happened to sex, the having of which, only a few short years before, was sought after as the Ultimate Experience, the sure way to self-expression and self-fulfillment, the cement to a rickety relationship, the nonstop route to happiness?

Hype strangled sex.

The media trivialized it.

Analysis annihilated its mystery.

One of life's most exquisite experiences has been so dissected, so discussed, made so explicit, mechanical, and overdone that people are saying it's *boring!*

"Sex became too commercial. It was overvalued commercially and undervalued emotionally," sums up a thoughtful Los Angeles movie magnate whom I interviewed. "The things in sex that have always been permeated with a sense of discovery became clichés instead."

"Anxiety caused the cool-off on sex," observes a New York therapist. "The tremendous emphasis on *performance,* on doing it right, made a lot of people nervous. Who would dare admit that they were sexually insecure? After all, you're *supposed* to know how to be a terrific lover, you're supposed to have had multiple orgasms and to know how to give fantastic oral sex. We read about insatiable women with tidal-wave orgasms and superstuds with nonstop erections. People think that what's going on in everyone *else's* bedroom is unbelievably exciting, so it's not surprising that they become anxious about what's going on behind their own closed doors. Fear and anxiety are still the biggest sexual turn-offs."

"I think I know by now how to push all the buttons and find all the right triggers," counters a good-looking twenty-eight-year-old graphics designer from Victoria, Texas, who admits he is a victim of a new sexual lethargy, "but just keeping track of all those things becomes a burden and deadens your responses instead of firing them up. I'm just not so turned on anymore."

Is it possible to regenerate and rekindle old-fashioned, exciting, wicked feelings like lust and overwhelming desire? What does it take to make sex a wonderful, magical, marvelous adventure instead of a laborious task? What's going to make sex sexy again?

WHERE DO WE GO FROM HERE?

That's what this book is all about.

CHAPTER 2

What's Great Sex?

WHAT IS "GREAT SEX" and what's so great about it?

Great sex takes place *between men and women who are individuals and who are equals.* It doesn't assume that the man—or woman—automatically takes the lead or has most of the responsibility.

Great sex goes *beyond mechanics* and is involved with total pleasure—physically, emotionally, spiritually. Great sex takes us beyond the basics, *without all the anxiety and fears of performance.*

Great sex always uses your most important sex organ—*the brain.*

Great sex is between two people, not just two bodies. It's an *understanding of the other person,* it's sex with that most overused, least practiced word: communication.

Great sex is *intense, passionate, magical.* Great sex is, above all, *sex-with-love-and-romance.*

I think Anaïs Nin, a writer with profound understanding of the sexes and a penchant for exquisite erotica, put it best when she wrote, "Only the united beat of sex and heart together can create ecstasy." (Anaïs Nin, *Delta of Venus,* 1969)

Mae West said it in her own inimitable style: "Honey, sex with love is the greatest thing in life, but sex without love—that's not so bad either." Today, very few people are experiencing the greatest thing in life, much less a distant second best—and this is strongly confirmed by statistical evidence. To use just one example, a recent article in the *New England Journal of Medicine* described a study of one hundred "happily married couples" that found that 50 percent of the men and a whopping 77 percent of the women were having sex problems. Many other studies could be cited that show the same results.

One of the most common reasons for this widespread discontent is simply lack of knowledge. Mae West again: "Men were so surprised by me, I knew there must be a lot of women out there doing it badly. Or maybe not doing it bad enough." (Quoted in Charlotte Chandler, *The Ultimate Seduction,* 1984)

Mae's observation holds true today. The number of men and women who say that their husbands/ wives/lovers *still* don't know how to make love to them is astonishing. Even with the sophisticated information that's so readily available, romantic, wonderful, wicked sex is something many people have never experienced—though they are usually too embarrassed to admit it.

Thus, one of the aims of this book is to give the most specific, up-to-date research in the field, for sexual literacy is the best antidote to the fears, prejudices, guilt, and apprehensions that still abound in bedrooms across the country. And, although many people just don't like to hear it, technique *is* important. Very often I hear people say, "Oh, that technique talk is just so much hooey. It makes sex sound so clinical and mechanical." I suspect that this kind of response comes from never having experienced a really knowledgeable lover or from the fear that one is ignorant oneself.

You can knock a ball with a tennis racquet and you'll probably get it over the net, but if you have a few pointers your game is going to improve enormously. The same goes for sex: You were born with the instinct of reproducing the species, but you weren't born with the specific knowledge of how to give someone else pleasure. If you don't know what you're doing or how to do it, you're missing out on some of the most marvelous experiences a human can have.

How does all this specific, physiological/biological/technique stuff jibe with the idea of romantic, exciting, great sex? Won't it get us right back to where we started? Overdoing, overexplaining, overexposing what should be magical and mysterious? There *are* more wondrous, marvelous mysteries in sex than in anything else, but to truly and fully enjoy them you first need knowledge and information. It's only then that you can soar into a sexual stratosphere you might never have known existed.

This book starts where *Joy of Sex* and its followers left off. The material you'll find on the following pages comes from extensive research on the latest information on sexuality as well as from interviews with a broad range of expert sources: sociologists, psychologists, physicians, sex therapists, marriage counselors, pastoral counselors, and sex researchers. I've tried to translate—and simplify—clinical terminology and therapeutic techniques into language that's both clear and understandable.

But that's only part of what *Great Sex* is about.

We all need and respond to new, fresh ideas. Many of us are looking for easy, fast-action ways to climb out of a sexual sluggishness and make so-so sex into something a lot more intriguing. Everyone I know, including myself, would be interested in discovering some new turn-ons to make sex not just good but *great.*

And that's what the other part of this book deals with.

When I wrote *How to Make Love to a Man* and *How to Make Love to Each Other,* I was especially careful not to use titillating or erotic material because I felt that my purpose was simply to deliver the straightforward information that men and women still found unavailable.

This book is different. For example, the story of Michael and Diana that is threaded through these pages is included because *it is intended to be physically arousing* as well as entertaining. Clear, specific, technical information is also interwoven with suggestions, scenarios, and seductions that I found to be fresh, fun, outrageous, wonderful—and useful.

Most of this material came from interviews that I did on my many trips crisscrossing the country. The men and women whom I talked with (over 200) came from all educational, ethnic, and geographical backgrounds, and they had new tips, ideas, and fascinating erotic tales to tell. Some of this material will, I hope, turn you on. Other ideas may not be your cup of tea, but what I'm trying to do is provide takeoff points— the ultimate destination is of course whatever you both wish it to be.

Great sex must be more than physical—it needs laughter, tears, fantasies, and dreams. The idea that should permeate this book is that the infinite power of sex comes from feeling, passion, curiosity, mood, and invention.

CHAPTER 3

Who's Sexy Now?

I REMEMBER a time when the big, brand-name stars radiated sexual heatwaves right off the silver screen. Almost everyone who watched movies agreed that the likes of Marlon, Marilyn, Newman, and Sophia were Hot, Hot, Hot—no matter how cool they played it. As visions of these charged sexual presences flashed through my mind, I thought that compiling an informal list of "Who's Sexy Now" would be amusing and perhaps even helpful in determining what "sexy" is all about in the eighties.

29

The minute you ask "Who do you think is sexy?" you'll find you've sparked a heated discussion. A few minutes' talk will probably include some of the superstars who now come in androgynous packages. Then you're likely to hear much speculation about the vast spectrum of today's highly public personalities—and a surprising number and variety of these are considered HOT. Although I had more discussions on the subject than I care to remember, the bottom line is that it is almost impossible to assemble any sort of definitive list of who the big turn-ons are today.

Since I could find no consensus on who's really and truly SEXY, I changed the question a bit. "What makes a person sexy?" I began asking.

"If someone acts as if she or he is attractive even though they're not, then people are attracted to that person. I've seen it happen over and over again," said the sexy editor in chief of a major women's magazine as we lunched on sushi in a hushed Japanese restaurant. "You know," she added, "I remember being at a party and hearing Helen Gurley Brown say to someone she'd just met, 'What did you do today?' It's such an intimate question to ask, and it makes the other person feel that you're so interested in him—*that's* sexy!"

"A woman who is not defensive about sex is truly sexy," said a New York deal-making lawyer in his office high up in the Helmsley Building. "She lets you know she's interested and that she *likes* sex. She puts up no emotional or physical defenses or barriers."

"I date a woman who is the office manager in a very busy firm," said a sandy-haired man as he repaired my word processor. "She would plan all day what to wear when I was going to her house for dinner. She would plan where to place the chairs, what kind of music I'd like. When she told me that she was thinking all these things, I'd get a great smile on my face. She doesn't have a particularly good figure, she isn't beautiful, and she's very short—but she really knows how to make someone feel good. That's what I think makes a sexy person—male or female."

"There's a lot of different 'sexies,'" says the high-energy, dark-haired executive producer of a successful national television show geared for women. "But basically it means a person who knows who he or she is, someone who has a strong awareness of themself and a confidence in what they're doing."

This man's answer to the question "What makes a person sexy?" is one version of a response I heard over and over and over again—from both men and women. Here are other ways of putting it:

Sexy is self-confident.

Sexy is self-assured.

Sexy means having faith in one's powers without being conceited or arrogant.

Sexy means feeling good about yourself—body and soul.

Nine out of every ten people I probed ultimately came up with some version of "self-confidence," but there were other interesting areas of agreement about what makes a person sexy or desirable.

"A man or woman who lets you know they're interested in sensuality is sexy. You can tell by the way they look at you—straight in the eye; by the way they touch you—lingeringly, but not a second too long; and sometimes by the way they dress. They let you know that sex is a priority with them, but always with great subtlety. If they were obvious, they wouldn't be sexy," comments a radio news reporter in Detroit.

"Someone who's passionate is sexy," declares a writer from Hartford, Connecticut. "There is heat and intensity and curiosity in passion—any kind of passion. People are usually consistent in their personalities; a person who's passionate about ideas is usually wonderful in bed. I'm sick and tired of 'cool.' A man or woman who's cool is probably going to be cool about everything—including sex."

Passion—an intimate sexual abandon—says Dr. Otto Kernberg, the distinguished psychoanalyst, can provide "an internal wildness that preserves marriage." (Interview, *New York Times*, November 20, 1984)

You may disagree with some or all of these opinions, but one area where there seems to be almost no disagreement involves attractiveness. Physical attractiveness, for the majority of men and women, is sexy. This doesn't mean having a beautiful face, perfectly formed breasts, gorgeously delineated muscles, or an adorable behind. It's obviously a plus if God gave you some specially delectable physical attributes, but very few of us are born totally beautiful. Having a cared-for body—meaning healthy and fit and well-groomed—is absolutely basic when it comes to being sexy.

"Most of us can't compete with movie stars," says the crackerjack secretary to a Manhattan patent attorney, "but when you take care of yourself and look your maximum, you feel good about yourself." And that's exactly the message I've been trying to get across—when you feel good/confident/attractive, you feel sexy, you *transmit* sexy.

One of the most memorable comments that I heard on the subject of looking good came from a Parisian who works in a boutique on New York's fashionable 57th Street. "When I hear a woman lament about not being attractive enough, I tell her straightaway what Coco Chanel once said: 'There are no ugly women, only lazy ones.' And don't tell me you don't have the time: after all, what does it take to shave your legs and have smooth, soft skin—sixty seconds?"

CHAPTER 4

September, Italy

MICHAEL WAS SCHEDULED to leave Paris for New York, and Diana, as planned, was flying south to Italy. Early on Monday morning, when Diana was taking a bath, she heard Michael placing a call. From the businesslike tone of his voice, Diana assumed he was calling his office. Then he hung up and dialed again. This time his words were soft and intimate. Instinctively she knew he was talking to a woman. An unexpected dart of jealousy sniped at her. She rose from the bathtub, hurriedly dried herself.

She was taken completely by surprise when Michael burst into the bathroom, a suitcase in each hand.

"Pack your bags," he fairly shouted. "We're going to Rome! I don't have to be at the office until Thursday. We have three days to enjoy the marvels of Italy!"

"Now what if I told you I was meeting a lover in Rome?" Diana asked teasingly.

"You told me the night we met that you'd be alone in Europe," he said evenly, carefully setting the bags down on the white tile floor. "I thought you'd like some company, but perhaps I'm mistaken." Suddenly he was very serious. "Maybe you want to be alone, or with someone else, and I'm just intruding on your plans. I don't like to play games."

"Michael, it was unbelievably dumb of me to say that. You know I'd like nothing better than to go to Rome with you. I don't know why I said something so stupid."

Keep cool, she counseled herself once again, you're always so *intense.* She wanted to keep this trip light and easy, but everything was happening so fast that she was afraid she might be falling in love with Michael. His phone call a few minutes ago had thrown her—who was he talking to so intimately?

Why, she wondered, angry at herself, *why couldn't she just say, It's a fabulous adventure, a wonderful fantasy-come-true. Why couldn't she just say, I'm in this for a good time with my body.* Even with a man she barely knew, she was already playing out a love scene.

"We've got to be on the plane in a little over an

hour. We've got to *move!*" Michael said, dissipating the small cloud of tension.

They reached the airport in record time, dashed for the plane. In a short hour they had landed in Rome. Diana could hardly catch her breath, nor did she really want to. All the mad rush and fuss with tickets, passports, and luggage made the trip feel even more adventurous.

The wild taxi ride into the heart of the city further heightened the excitement. The Fiat careened around corners, the driver shouting and shaking his fist at the universal incompetence of everyone else but himself.

"Where are we going?" she asked Michael, holding on to him for dear life, realizing that they didn't have hotel reservations.

"It's all taken care of," he said, putting his arms around her. They had reached a circular piazza, and small cars were coming at them like cannonballs from every direction, but the driver maintained his pace. Diana closed her eyes.

Miraculously the Fiat navigated the treacherous whorl of traffic and screeched to a halt on the narrowest of cobblestone streets.

They were in front of the hotel where she had planned to stay, a small, charming place several short blocks from the foot of the famous Spanish Steps.

"You'd mentioned the name of this hotel to me, and luckily I remembered it. Since I've never been in Rome, I thought it would be best to follow your choice," he said.

Their lovely high-ceilinged room had a small stucco balcony with two wrought-iron chairs that gave onto a back courtyard. Just below was a tile roof and another terrace crowded with enormous terra-cotta pots of geraniums.

"Let's not even unpack, lets *go!*" said Michael, effortlessly picking her up and twirling her around on the small balcony.

She loved that boundless energy and enthusiasm.

"Follow me!" Diana said, laughing and pulling him by the hand. "Even though I was here six years ago I think I can find a place you'll like."

She headed straight for the elegant Via Condotti and a place that had been a favorite of hers: the Cafe Greco. The white-haired waiter took their order: pungent Roman espresso and croissants lightly laced with orange. They lingered over a second cup of coffee and decided that after all the rushing they'd spend the rest of the morning just walking with no particular destination.

. It was early autumn and the air was exhilaratingly dry and clear. At lunchtime they found they were near a small trattoria that Diana had heard was famous for its porcini mushrooms, those big white treasures of Italy that were right in season.

The restaurant itself was enchanting. They sat in an ancient cobblestoned courtyard under a green and white striped awning with ivy twining up the cables that held it in place. They started with pasta, then relished the porcini, which tasted like a delicate kind of meat, sampled a wonderfully green and leafy salad, and finished with a spectacular chestnut cake layered with whipped cream and crushed almonds.

"I simply can't resist Italian food," Diana announced ruefully to Michael, who never, it seemed, had to count calories.

After lunch Diana suddenly announced, "I have an absolutely crazy idea!" Their energy seemed so boundless and their senses so receptive to every stimulus that she wanted to do and see and taste even more. "Let's go to Florence tomorrow! We can see the Vatican museum this afternoon and take the morning train tomorrow. Then we can come back tomorrow night and still have another day in Rome before you leave. What do you think? Is it too crazy to do all that?"

Of course it was crazy, but it was agreed on in a minute. They would drive their senses mad with pleasure. They'd see all the great works of art in the Uffizi galleries, they'd explore the marvels of Florence, they'd search for the famous white truffles which were just coming into season, they'd look at the shops filled with wonderful things—and they'd do it all in one day!

Michael fell in love with Florence.

Diana was falling in love with Michael. She told herself not to spoil things by getting serious. Enjoy it for what it is: a magical affair. But she couldn't fool herself: it was more to her than that.

They were recharging from the morning at the Uffizi by having cappucino and gelati in a small cafe.

"I wanted to find you something as a remembrance from Florence," Michael said. "Maybe you'd like . . ."

"Oh, no, Michael. You've done too much already. Anyway, we don't have time to shop. We've got to see the Michelangelo 'David' this afternoon. That is really a high point and we can't miss it. The best present I can have is to see your reaction."

"Okay, of course we'll go there. Why don't we walk? The exercise will feel good."

Michelangelo's "David," as predicted, was the pinnacle of a unique day. Michael seemed to respond to sculpture even more than to painting. Perhaps, she mused, it was because his own body was so beautiful.

"I think I might be tired," Michael admitted as they tried in vain to find a taxi to take them to the station.

"Me too. It's too much to take in in such a short time."

"Why don't we spend the night here and go back to Rome in the morning? We can take a nap and find a special place for dinner."

"Perfect idea. And I even know of a place to stay."

They agreed it was their lucky day. The hotel had one room left. They bought Italian toothbrushes, shaving cream, a razor—they loved having Italian things to use—and settled in.

Laughing, wrestling, they fell on the bed. Michael started kissing her and rolling them over and over. She felt him hard on top of her, the full weight of his body pushing down on hers.

"I want you," he said in a low, urgent voice as he quickly unbuckled his belt.

The deep red skin had pulled tightly over his hard, swollen penis. He saw the spreading wetness on her bikini pants as he tore them off. His middle finger, sure of its target, moved deep into her vagina, probing, searching, pressing, gliding in and out with a slow, firm, even rhythm. Another finger found the rigid nub that made her whole body pulsate.

Slowly, tantalizingly, while the hand held her lower lips apart, his hard tongue moved down her body and began to stroke her clitoris with small catlike flicks. Her breasts swelled, her head was suddenly dizzy, and invisible currents were building to an explosion between her legs.

Her pelvis began to move rhythmically back and forth as his tongue relentlessly moved over the center of her being. She opened her mouth, she opened her legs, she seemed to have millions of openings, every inflamed cell of her body wanted him to penetrate her.

The climax was coming. She was sliding, circling, rising, swirling, when suddenly he was entering her with deep, hard thrusts, into the deepest places of her womb, touching the most hidden nerves of her response. As he pushed inside her, his fingers were rolling and pinching her nipples in the same quickening rhythm of his thrusting. His voice, repeated over and over in a low, driving, guttural tone, "Yes, yes, yes, yes . . ."

He gripped her ankles and threw her legs over his shoulders and began to move his throbbing, pulsating penis even deeper as her body undulated to meet the piercing thrusts. And then he arched his back for a long, charged moment, every muscle in his powerful torso thrown into sharp relief, "Yes, ooohh, yeesssss . . ."

His golden chest had flushed to a deep coppery color in the late afternoon light. His taut, polished skin was streaked with sweat. He fell back exhausted, his eyes closed, his breathing slowly becoming even and signaling sleep.

When they woke it was close to nine and they realized that if they didn't hurry they'd have no dinner— a not-to-be-missed event. The concierge told them of a small trattoria tucked into a picturesque alley a few steps in from the Arno. It was one of the best meals they had in Italy. They lingered over wild strawberries as they talked about the bounty of Florence.

"I feel as if I belong here," Michael said thoughtfully. "I must come back."

"I"—not "we." That hurt.

To be continued . . .

CHAPTER 5

How to Beat Sexual Gridlock

"A LOT OF MEN say they want love, but they really mean sex," commented a young blond woman who was sitting in the front row of the Phil Donahue show, which we were taping in Chicago. Her observation is one with which many women would agree.

What's behind the double message? The answer lies in what I call a man's dual attitude toward sex.

Men's and women's attitudes about love are very *similar,* but when it comes to sex they have very different conceptions and expectations. Women often confuse sex with love. The majority of women want an element of caring and affection in a sexual experience. "Sex is high priority for me," says a successful hair stylist from New York. "I've probably been involved in the numbers game as much as men, and although I've been to bed with a lot of men on a casual basis I recently realized that I've almost always hoped that something romantic would develop. Men can have sex without expectations."

She's right. Most men do have a different viewpoint: sometimes they want sex with love and sometimes they want to have pure physical sex. Often a man is himself unaware of this duality in his thinking.

One level of a man's sexual experience is what we usually refer to as "making love." Making love, as I'm using the words here, involves two people who can reach as high as they want to emotionally and physically. Making love involves caring, warmth, sensitivity, nurturing—and the physical acts of sex (which may or may not include intercourse). When you have made love there is an enveloping feeling of intimacy and love.

"Making love—what you call 'great sex'—is totally consuming," a male graduate student at Columbia University said to me. "Just 'having sex' is a pleasant physical diversion." As other men I interviewed defined it, "having sex" can be a way to relieve physical/sexual tension or to work out emotions that can range from anger and frustration to sadness and grief. "It makes you feel better—temporarily," is how one man summed it up. This kind of sex can be casual to the point of impersonal, and what your partner does or doesn't do is often irrelevant; it's usually a totally self-oriented activity. Some women *do* compartmentalize sexual experience into loving sex or casual sex, but they are a small minority.

A woman who says "He just wants me for my body" may be right on target. He may simply want pure physical sex, no emotional strings attached. "When you're more involved with a man than he is with you, you want desperately to hear he cares," says a writer I know. "So sometimes he feels forced to say, 'I love you.' You can sense the words sound hollow, but you *want* to believe him so you have sex with him and then feel used." What follows is, naturally, bewilderment and resentment.

"I believe that you've got to be up-front with a woman when you're in it just for sex," says a sensitive single man. "Tender words can be an open-sesame to a woman's body, but it's obviously manipulative to say things that you don't mean. I once told a woman who really attracted me that I enjoyed her company and wanted to go to bed with her but I wasn't ready for a relationship. Although I knew she was very interested in me, she turned down the sex. I know I missed out on a good thing by being so honest, but I've found it's the only way to avoid emotional pitfalls."

Understanding that each of you may want different things from a sexual relationship is another way to detour emotional minefields. But it *is* possible for both of you to be satisfied. When a man wants a direct physical/sexual release, it certainly doesn't have to result in feelings of loneliness or emptiness for a woman. The sheer raw power of purely physical sex can be terrifically exciting when a woman is with someone she cares for and that someone reciprocates with warm, caring lovemaking when she needs it.

The Great Love/Sex Gridlock

The confusion of love and sex is the prime reason behind what I've called "sexual gridlock"—those constantly crossed wires that we encounter in our relationships with the opposite sex. There's no possibility of good sex—much less anything of a higher order— unless we begin to unblock the sexual logjam.

Much of the problem is caused by the fact that most of us are still locked in stereotyped roles. By 1984 the macho man and the passive woman should have been relegated to the psychological junkheap, but this is far from a reality. The media would have us think that the new trend in sex is for women to make first moves. Do you know of a woman who has kissed a man before he's kissed her? The widespread feeling is *still* that it's unbecoming for a woman to be too sexually assertive. A frustrated friend of mine sums it up this way: "It's the old double-standard: our society says that women are unfeminine if they express lust, but men are not men if they don't."

Research confirms this. Men and women are still strongly encouraged to pursue different sexual goals—the man initiating and the woman setting the limits. Further, if a man initiates too soon, he's coming on too strong, and if he waits too long, he's passive, unexciting, or probably gay.

In a recent experiment on what men and women will/won't disclose it was found that women do not reveal their strengths and men fear telling their weaknesses. The fact that women still hide their skills so they won't be threatening to men, and the fact that men are still fearful of exposing their vulnerability, goes a long way to explain why the traditional roles of the "strong, silent type" and the "sweet little woman" remain with us.

Another interesting report that explores male/female relationships (C. S. Kirkpatrick, in *Psychology of Women Quarterly,* Spring 1980) shows that couples who followed "traditional sex-role stereotypes seemed to have greater difficulty resolving their sexual problems than less role-distinct couples." And equally as revealing is the fact that women who rate high as "feminists" (meaning that they endorsed statements of equality between the sexes) masturbated more, were more orgasmic, and more aroused by erotic stimuli. And these same women tended to initiate sex as frequently as their partners did. The bottom line: Women who rate high as feminists have more sexual satisfaction.

Where does all this information lead us? Directly, I

think, to mixed messages and mass confusion about what it means to be a man or woman today. And this kind of confusion drives us straight to sexual gridlock.

Perhaps the most interesting—and important—research on differences between males and females has been done by psychologist Carole Gilligan at Harvard. Her findings, I think, point the way to understanding the basic causes of gridlock.

Her work elucidates why the majority of women need to experience sex with closeness and affection, while men can experience sex as a casual, impersonal physical experience. It explains why women need to talk things out and men don't want to communicate. To put it in a different way, Gilligan's observations clarify why a man may be thinking "OH, WOW! HOT SEX!" when she's thinking "OH, GREAT! IT'S GOING TO BE LOVE AND INTIMACY!" or why a woman is thinking "COMMUNICATION BETWEEN US WILL SOLVE THE PROBLEM," when he's saying to himself, "WHY CAN'T SHE JUST LEAVE ME ALONE!"

At the risk of vastly oversimplifying her exceptional insights, Gilligan says in brief that women are nurturers. We place a high value on relationships and are threatened by separation, while men need autonomy and are threatened by intimacy. Men, Gilligan points out, see danger in connection while women experience danger in separation. And this, I think, explains the underlying structure of sexual gridlock.

Getting Out of Gridlock

Some psychologists and researchers claim that androgyny is the way out of sexual gridlock. ("Androgyny," as I'm using it here, has nothing to do with how a person looks or what her or his sexual preferences are.) One argument suggests that the psychologically androgynous person is free from the stereotyped role-playing and cultural conditioning that causes so much frustration. Such a person can enjoy a richer and fuller life, since he or she is equally comfortable with masculine and feminine responses. In fact, some experts have said that androgynous qualities may be just the right stuff for future astronauts who are required to spend increasing amounts of time in the stressful, constricted environments of space capsules. In several tests people who were emotionally and intellectually considered androgynous were rated as having more self-esteem, the corollary to this being the higher one's self-esteem the more satisfactory his/her sex life.

This is an interesting line of thought, and androgyny is ultimately the best way to end the battle of the sexes, but I think right now that's pushing the envelope too far. Most of us aren't ready for full-fledged androgyny—yet.

But what then is going to break the gridlock, help uncross the high-tension wires, and melt the wall that still separates the sexes?

The answers lie in understanding, awareness—and sex.

First, take sex. Paradoxical as it might sound, sex itself can be the biggest key to solving a great many of the sexual standoffs that we experience. If sex is good, it's going to help break up the gridlock. Most people believe that a good relationship makes for good sex, but many therapists are reversing gears—sex comes first and *then* the relationship improves. Sex opens up the barricades, makes you more willing to work on the trouble spots in the relationship. In an interview (*Ms.*, February 1984) writer Marge Piercy sums up what many men and women feel: "When I have good sex with someone, I put up with more and am infinitely more motivated to work out problems. When someone withdraws sexually—a great way to manipulate a partner who likes sex—then already part of the motivation for getting through the muck is diminished."

But for sex to be good or even great—and that's the kind of sex that breaks down barriers and eases the sexual traffic jam—it takes trust, awareness, and understanding of the other person. You should know that his/her expectations, hang-ups, and attitudes are different from yours. If you keep in mind that men can truly fear intimacy (although they may want it badly) and that women need loving relationships, it is easier to see why he or she may be acting a certain way that up to now hasn't made a bit of sense to you.

And, ultimately, remember that sameness can be stultifying. If we all had the exact same ideas and feelings and attitudes we'd be bland as processed cheese—and sex *would* be truly boring. Where we differ—emotionally and physically—we can value those differences instead of seeing them as stumbling blocks. What can you offer the other person that is new, that he or she doesn't already know? Michael Korda (in *Self*, November 1983) sums it up this way: "In the best relationships we are always learning something new and surprising about the other person and therefore inevitably about ourselves. We are, to put it simply, growing."

CHAPTER 6

P.A.—What No One Likes to Talk About

IN THE PAST DECADE all the emphasis on Doing It, Doing It Right, and Doing It A Lot took away much of the joy of sex and gave men—and now women—a rattling good case of "performance anxiety" as it is called by the sex therapists. No one likes to talk about P.A., but it is one of the biggest fears that sabotages sex.

"A guy will quickly tell you that Isabel or Veronica or Sabra is a lousy lay," says a thirty-six-year-old New

York entertainment lawyer who has just embarked on a postseparation sexual bender. "But have you ever heard someone wonder if *he* might be the one who's not so great in the sack? Sure I'm worried about how I stack up, but I'm never going to say it. I'd tell a lot of people a lot of things before I'd say I was worried about getting it up."

What is a man's greatest sexual fear?

Performance, performance, performance.

No matter how young or how old, no matter how good a lover—*and no matter what he tells you*—*every* man is worried about performing in bed. Even though we've heard and read so much about how women are taking the lead sexually, a *man still feels that he's the one in charge* and if he doesn't perform, if his penis does not harden, *his masculinity is at stake.*

And if he's with a woman who is coming on to him, who is sending out sexual signals, he may feel flattered, but on a deeper level he may feel anxious—he is *expected* to satisfy her. Most men have heard or read that it's not necessary to have an erection to "satisfy" a woman, but in their heart of hearts they don't believe it. Thus, to most men, satisfying her means coming up with a nonstop erection and giving her at least one orgasm.

Coming up with an erection is *the* root problem. "A man doesn't get a hard-on just because he desires one," explains the lawyer quoted above. "There is no worse feeling than wanting to have an erection when your cock won't cooperate. You feel helpless, out of control, and that's just the opposite of what every man wants when he's having sex."

The New Victims of Performance Shock

Until the advent of the orgasm with a capital O, women did not have to face the same fears about performance as men. We were expected to do nothing much more in bed than lie back and smile encouragingly. But by the height of the sexual revolution in the mid-seventies, female performance—having orgasm(s)—was a new and alarming issue. There was something wrong if we didn't experience a toe-tingling climax almost every time. And so just when we were learning to enjoy our own sexuality, we were forced to fake orgasm not only to assure our lovers that they were terrific, but to show them that we too were operating at peak performance.

Linked to female performance-anxiety is *oral sex,* which in recent years has become a measure of a woman's gifts in bed. "I know this may sound controversial," says an assistant in a SoHo art gallery, "but I think many men judge a woman on how she gives head. There's a double bind involved. If she's bad then she loses points, but if she's good he may wonder if she's promiscuous."

"If a woman goes down on me without my asking, I tend to think of her as liberated—but it's amazing how few women know how to do it right," reports a

Long Island building contractor, forty-five and divorced for two years. Although many people today assume that oral sex is about as common as kissing, there are a great many men and women who still have all kinds of problems with it. (Much more about oral sex in upcoming chapters.)

Body image is another aspect of performance anxiety which few women escape. We worry about stretchmarks, cellulite, drooping breasts, and a myriad of other minor imperfections. In short, the big anxiety is that we aren't *desirable* enough.

How to Beat Performance Anxiety

How can we cope with the pressures of performance, the anxieties of body image, and the fears of being rejected, looking ridiculous, not measuring up? Recent psychological studies in a surprising variety of areas provide some helpful answers.

You become anxious about performance when you consciously think about performing. It's like walking down stairs: Usually you just do it. But if you stop to think about each step, you are more likely to trip and perhaps fall. The same is true of sexual performance when you say to yourself, "I must have a rock-hard erection," or, "It's taking me so long to reach orgasm." In essence you're putting pressure on yourself, judging your performance. Psychologists call this *spectatoring*, and they point out that this is exactly what subverts sexual pleasure. The opposite of spectatoring is abandoning yourself, letting go, just *feeling* what is happening moment by moment.

Easy to say, but for some people very hard to do.

"You might want to look at it as a right brain/left brain situation," says a sports psychologist who has an interesting new viewpoint on performance anxiety. "The left brain observes, criticizes, judges; the right brain works on intuition, mental images, emotion. In athletics an important principle is the suppression of the verbal self and the encouragement of the visualizing self. Problems crop up when an athlete tries to control the physical responses of the right brain with the critical faculty of the left brain. During training you can criticize your efforts, but when you're actually performing—running the race—you want to let the right brain take over. We have made terrific strides in mental training with athletes, and much of this can be put to use in many other areas of life." Very definitely including sex, I would add. The man or woman who is anxious about performing first needs to know what to do. Then he or she must relax, abandon the critical, anxious spectatoring self, *feel* the body responding—and enjoy.

You *can* beat performance anxiety by relaxing. That's why warm baths, showers, and massages are highly recommended by sex therapists. Some of the new techniques suggested by psychologists, and especially sports psychologists, are equally as helpful, if not more so.

The following steps toward relaxation include a synthesis of the latest techniques. They take about fifteen minutes and can be done with your lover or alone.

To be successful, any relaxation system must show the differences between tension and relaxation. So first lie on your back, feet slightly apart, and rest your hands palms down.

Clench one fist. Be aware only of your *feelings.* Focus on the feelings in your fist, your hand, your forearm, your upper arm. Now relax your fist. Shake it out, relax it again. Now clench your fist once more. *Don't think* about what you're doing, simply *concentrate on the clenched sensations as intensely as you can.*

Relax your fist again. Shake it out. Relax completely. Don't think about relaxing, again *concentrate* on the *feelings of relaxation* in your fist, your hand, your forearm.

Remember, you are not performing these motions—you are simply feeling them.

Now the full body relaxation process begins.

Clench your feet as you clenched your fist. *Feel* the sensations intensely. Now relax your feet. *Feel* these sensations. Now move on to your ankles, tightening/clenching and then relaxing totally. Continue on to your

lower legs	abdomen
upper legs	shoulders
thighs	upper arms
buttocks	lower arms
lower back	hands
upper back	fists/fingers

Finally concentrate on your neck, your mouth, your nose, your eyes, your whole head, each time tensing and relaxing. When you have tensed and relaxed your entire body, stay in the relaxed position for two to four minutes, keeping your mind focused only on the feelings of relaxation. A warm body is also important to relaxing: you may find it helpful to imagine that you are in a warm place or that you are immersed in warm water.

The second half of outsmarting performance anxiety involves a right-brain skill and is a technique known as *visualizing.*

Visualizing is simply creating images in your brain. An athlete who uses this technique may visualize *in detail* the moves he or she must make in order to win a race or score a point. Visualizing, ultimately, is a method to inspire *confidence* in performance. You can apply this method to sex in a very simple way—it's really a more consciously oriented kind of fantasizing.

The point here is to visualize a positive sexual experience. You might start by imagining a room with the kinds of furnishings you like most. Note all the details so that the room becomes very clear to you. Next imagine your partner—it may be your lover, your usual partner, or a stranger. You can make up whatever scenario turns you on. Again visualize all the details as clearly as you can. Next imagine touching your partner, your partner touching you. *Feel* the touch, *feel* the skin you're touching. Continue slowly, imagining a complete sexual experience where you are giving and receiving the kinds of stimulation that you most want, again concentrating totally on the *feelings* and the pleasure of each of your physical movements, and those of your partner.

Visualizing a wonderful sexual experience in advance, say the therapists who practice these new techniques, gives you a highly useful tool to beat and defeat anxiety and fear. Visualizing is also erotically exciting—meaning it's a turn-on—and the short time that it takes to do these exercises is indeed well spent.

Note: The most comprehensive and complete relaxation and visualizing techniques that I found in my research are in Charles Garfield's *Peak Performance Sports* (published by J. P. Tarcher, Los Angeles, 1984), a book very much worth reading.

CHAPTER 7

The Hottest Spots

OUR MOST SENSITIVE AREAS are the erogenous zones—those delicious hot spots that, when kissed, stroked, rubbed, caressed, literally make your body warm with desire.

"The *entire* body—not just the breasts and genitals—is pleasure territory," points out one of the marriage counselors I interviewed, "but it still surprises me how few people make use of this fact. You can have an incredibly erotic experience by sucking someone's fingers or toes. The allusion to oral sex is obvious, and it can be enormously seductive."

Responses in erogenous areas differ according to a person's physical and psychological makeup, but love-producing sensitivity can be developed in almost any part of the body. Before we go on to the latest post-G-spot information about the hottest spots, here are a few thoughts on how to touch those tender areas suggested by some men and women I've interviewed.

What Drives Women Crazy

"Touch is half of what sensational sex is all about. It drives me crazy when a man doesn't know how to touch different parts of me. It's the biggest physical turn-off I can think of," says a Connecticut real estate broker. And most women would agree with her.

"Men that I love have an open hand," says a very attractive thirty-two-year-old day-care-center director. "They have a range of touch from very soft to very firm. There's no hesitation in the caress of a man who finds it a pleasure to be with a woman."

Men seem to fall into five different categories when it comes to touch. Here are the types that cause the most discomfort.

- THE GRABBER. He makes short, staccato, demanding movements instead of unhurried, sensuous skin contact. He needs to know that consistent, gentle touching and stroking will get him much further than a furtive grab or an overt lunge.

STRAIGHT-TO-THE-POINTS. He zeros in on the breasts first and then follows a direct route to the clitoris. He seems to be unaware that delicious detours can be made on the way to his final destination. He also seems to be oblivious to the fact that he's touching a person, not a sex button. Much of the art of arousing a woman lies in knowing that her whole body can vibrate from slow, warm, even caresses.

SPEED-O. This man is racing the clock to get to orgasm—his own. He pecks here, he rubs there—these speedy token touches and gestures quickly identify a graduate of the slam-bam-thank-you-ma'am school which should have folded years ago.

THE HEAVYWEIGHT. This fellow has a heavy hand and a mechanical touch. He needs to know that a light, feathery touch is a good starting point; as a woman becomes more responsive the touch can become firmer—but never heavy.

HE WHO HESITATES . . . "You can tell immediately how much a man knows about women by the decisiveness of his hand. The fumbler is a common type. He's uncertain, hesitant, and I feel as if he doesn't know what he's doing—or, worse, that he doesn't want me," says an executive secretary from Scottsdale, Arizona.

Be indirect. Men usually take the direct route to the genitals because that's the kind of touching they themselves prefer. Indirectness is a virtue when you are caressing a woman. Don't automatically head for the obvious—the breasts and genitals. Take the time to make a circuitous route—her lips, her ears, her chest, her back, then her breasts—respecting her wishes if she signals that she'd like you to stop or change course.

The same applies to the genital area. This takes time, but extended time and touching is exactly what most women need to become fully aroused sexually. A woman's sexual buildup is slow and consistent, and if you stop, even for a few seconds, especially when you are stroking the clitoris, the rising feelings can flatten out almost instantly. Keep your movements light, even, and *unhurried* unless you know she prefers something else.

Indirectness, as I have mentioned, is a virtue when you're touching a woman, and nonsexual touching—simple skin-on-skin without sexual overtones—can, paradoxically, often lead a woman to lovemaking. Here's how one woman describes the way warmth and affection affect her sexually: "I love a man who can take a strand of hair and tuck it behind my ear. I love it if a man holds my head in both his hands or kisses the side of my forehead or presses my cheek with his. I may not have sex on my mind, but if my lover is warm and affectionate I can get physically very turned on to sex."

Don't do unto others. The old adage "Do unto others as you would have them do unto you" does *not* hold true sexually.

Men's bodies and women's bodies don't necessarily respond to the same touches and techniques. Whereas women say they like a light touch, men are often in the opposite camp. They want a woman to hold them firmly, to touch them directly and without hesitation on the genitals. A man's musculature is different and responds to a firmer pressure. "I was going crazy because it felt like a flea was holding my penis," reports one man. "I finally took her hand and wrapped it around me, then I wrapped my hand around hers and showed her exactly what I wanted. She told me she would fly off the bed if anyone ever touched her that way. I realized she was just giving me what *she* would have liked.

"People have to spend a lot of time touching, stroking, massaging," the man concluded. "You don't just suddenly decode someone. You have to touch to convey desirability, sensuality—and to detense."

The best way to find out what kind of touch your lover likes is to *ask*. If you're shy about asking directly, you might begin by suggesting a backrub or massage. Use a body lotion or baby oil (warm it in your hands first) and stroke in long, sensuous movements, asking while you are doing this what kind of stroke and pressure he or she prefers.

"Usually I offer a massage to a woman, and I start off by simply saying, 'I want to make this feel great for you; let me know exactly what feels good,'" says a sensitive cosmetics executive who has made love to many, many women. "As I'm doing it, I ask, 'How does this feel? Do you like more or less firmness, more or less pressure?'—and I just continue in the same way when I get to her breasts and clitoris. Of course I love a woman who reciprocates without my asking, but if she doesn't offer I say, 'Now I'd love you to do that to me.'"

Here's the Latest Information on What and Where Feels Terrific

Recently, several researchers have been concentrating on areas of erotic sensitivity and have collected some interesting new information. Here's a rundown on the hottest spots.

Underexplored. Both the ears and neck are underrated, often unexplored areas of arousal. Lightly circling the tender area behind the ear and the inner rims of the ears with the tongue and then slipping its point into the deepest part of the ear in small in/out movements is, according to many men and women, a subtle but charged turn-on. The muscles and tendons leading from the ears down the neck to the shoulders are also very responsive to gentle biting, stroking, or massaging.

Especially sensitive sites. The armpits are wonderfully erogenous zones in both men and women: to some people the body scent here is a major turn-on. Kneading or gently biting the muscle that leads down the side of the body from the armpit is highly erotic.

Nipples. The entire surface of the chest is a primary arousal area for most women, with the nipples being the most responsive. "A woman's breasts should always be handled with exquisite sensitivity and extended timing," says a highly experienced man who describes his winning ways: "Women have told me that I'm a good lover because I take so much time with the breasts. I like to kiss and stroke and caress the entire chest area. *I'm very slow.* By the time I've worked around to the nipples the woman is usually very wet and wanting more," he explains.

There are some women who report little or no sensitivity in the breasts or nipples, and this is perfectly normal. On the other side of the coin, a few women reach orgasm from breast stimulation alone. A professional athlete told me that this was how she found out more about her body sexually: "I was having a Swedish massage. Usually the masseuse or masseur leaves the breasts out, but this woman very unsexually started massaging and kneading my chest. I realized that I could really be turned on this way. I asked my boyfriend to do it and after a few seconds my breasts were really hard. When he started kissing and biting my nipples, I had a fantastic orgasm after just a few minutes."

About 60 percent of men have partial or full erection of their nipples when stimulated. Men report a slightly different sensation when their nipples are stimulated. From my understanding, the feeling seems to be more specific, more direct. "If she sucks or bites my nipples I feel it right away in my penis," is the way one man described it.

Often a man is unaware of the erotic potential of his nipples and at first may find the sensation mildly unpleasant. (Or he may even be embarrassed by his arousal, as was the case with this man: "I went out with a woman who was very skillful. When she first stimulated my chest I didn't like it—I associated it with a woman's turn-on.")

Using lotion to make contact more slippery heightens the sensation (this goes for women too) and the uncomfortable feeling quickly disappears.

The backside. The entire area of the buttocks and inner thighs responds to light biting and very firm kissing. Erotic highs can come from direct stimulation of the genitals while biting the area where the buttocks join the top of the legs. Also, lightly biting or kneading the tendons that lead down the inner thighs from the genital area (where your inner thighs would touch a saddle) can produce delicious sensations.

The erotic cushion. In women, the mons pubis, or, more romantically, the mound of Venus, lies about six inches below the navel and is covered by pubic hair. The best way to feel arousal here is through pressure. A medium to quite-firm pressure with the fingers or heel of your hand at the top of the pubic hair, extending downward about an inch or two, feels wonderful when combined with other manual/oral delights.

Some women report that applying rhythmic pressure or kneading this area for a minute or more contributes to a terrific orgasm. One woman described this technique clearly: "When he has the heel of his one hand there—at the ridge of the pelvic bone—and his thumb on my clitoris, and two fingers of his other hand are moving deep inside my vagina, I just can't stop coming."

The X zone: good news from the vagina. The entrance to the vagina is loaded with nerves and is highly sensitive to mouth or hand stimulation. Until research pinpointed the G spot, the *interior* of the vagina was considered pretty numb in terms of erotic potential. However, the most recent findings confirm that in many women the vagina does contain one or more erogenous spots which when stimulated can produce a most intense kind of orgasm.

In an interesting and rather unusual clinical experiment in Colombia, South America (*Journal of Sex and Marital Therapy,* Spring 1984), the vaginal walls of forty-eight women were stimulated with the index and/or middle finger. Forty-five women reported high erotic sensitivity located in most cases on the upper anterior (the front) wall of the vagina, and many of the women also reported the same intense erotic response on the back wall of the vagina. One woman described the sensation as "having a clitoris in her vagina."

For the purposes of clarity, and to differentiate

them from what's been called the G spot, I'll label these spots or areas X zones.

Don't expect to find your special spot or X zone with a brand-new lover: it takes time and intimacy to explore and investigate the deeper reaches of the vagina. But, according to the experts and women who report what it feels like to find this hot spot, the search is delicious and well worth the time. Not all women have responded to deep vaginal stimulation, but mounting evidence does show that G spots or X zones are indeed real for a considerable number of women.

The road to discovery involves the application of a firm, rhythmic pressure with the middle and/or index finger (lubricated with unfragranced body lotion or KY jelly) to the front wall of the vagina. The finger or fingers should be at a slight angle to the wall of the vagina in order to produce the most stimulating effect. Proceed from the lower half to the upper half of the vagina and then do the same thing along the rear wall until you feel an acute erotic sensation. At the location of that intensely concentrated feeling, apply increasing rhythmic pressure. If the rhythmic, stroking pressure continues, a woman will almost certainly go on to orgasm or multiple orgasms.

To note: Many women feel a slightly uncomfortable urge to urinate when their particular X zone is stimulated. As the stimulation continues, the urge goes away.

The pinnacle. Even though many women can be extremely aroused by deep vaginal stroking, the center of physical feeling for a woman still lies in the clitoris. Much ink has been spilled over this nub of intensity, but many men are still not knowledgeable of the delicacies involved in its arousal.

The clitoris erects and swells—the change may not be noticeable or it may enlarge to twice its size—when a woman is aroused. Like the penis, the clitoris has a head, or glans, which is its most sensitive part. The sides and shaft of the clitoris are also enormously responsive. Just before and during orgasm the clitoris disappears under a "hood," but it remains supremely sensitive, and stimulation should not be stopped—just continue by stroking the outer lips. The indirect touching is enough to continue to orgasm.

The clitoris is nestled in an area which is also enormously sensitive to touch. The smart lover knows that the more time taken with stimulation of the entire genital area, the more his partner will respond when he finally touches the clitoris itself.

One man graphically described this by saying, "What a woman really wants from sex is *time.* You don't touch her there right away. You work up to it, slowly, slowly, slowly. You start with touching, kissing, licking the inner thighs, and then you work up to the outer lips. If there's not enough lubrication, use body lotion. (I like Nutraderm—no smell, almost no taste, easy to find in drugstores.) Then you tease the mouth of the vagina with little in/out flicks of your finger or tongue. And then you work on the sides of the clitoris.

Every movement should be fluid. The key is, don't stop unless she requests it.

The penis—and some new measurements. Before going on to the physical sensitivity of the penis, a short digression on a sensitive subject might be enlightening for both men and women. Size is a big issue with men. A man rarely sees another man's erect penis, thus he may fantasize that other men's members are enormous. In its flaccid state, penis size does vary, but erection is the great equalizer. Approximately six inches was the size of an erect penis as charted by the Kinsey Institute for Sex Research between 1938 and 1963.

The most up-to-date information varies from the Kinsey data. In a report published in the spring of 1984, researchers John Money, Gregory Lehne, and Frantz Pierre-Jerome of Johns Hopkins used a sample of sixty-five healthy men and found that the average penis size was approximately six and one half inches. The longest penis measured was eight inches and the shortest four and a half.

The measurements were taken by having the subject grasp the glans of his penis between his thumb and first finger and then stretch the penis as far as he could along the underside of a 12-inch ruler held in position by the examiner on the top side of the penis. The end of the ruler was pushed as close to the pelvic bone as was feasible without hurting the subject.

Perhaps the most psychologically important studies about penises are the ones that have been conducted by any number of women's magazines in the past few years. This research—both formal and informal—confirms that although there seems to be a very small minority of women who are involved with the size of a man's penis, most women are not interested in epic proportions—the big thing is the man himself.

A penis may be beautifully curved or elegantly straight; it may veer to the left or the right. The angle at which it erects differs from man to man—some jut out at 45 degrees and others assume higher or lower angles.

All of the penis is highly responsive, but the most sensitive area is the head. The next most responsive spots are the ridge at the base of the head (just above where the head joins the shaft of the penis) and the delicate vertical thread of skin on the underside of the head where it joins the shaft. The long ridge, which can look like an engorged vein, that runs along the underside is also an area of high sensation.

When the penis is erect you can feel how deeply it extends into the body by pressing your fingers up into the area behind the scrotum (the sac that houses the testes, or balls); you'll find its base is near the rectum.

"You can't miss finding the root of the penis if you massage the area under the balls. One of the things that feels best is when my lover is going down on me and she strokes the area over the base of the penis in a back-and-forth horizontal motion," explains one man whom I interviewed. "Be sure to say," he added, "that it has to be done with a firm hand. What's going on with the head of your penis is so intense that you have to stroke the root pretty hard to get both feelings. But it really magnifies the way you come."

The place to watch. The skin of the scrotum responds to licking and kissing, also light blowing. As orgasm approaches, the skin condenses and thickens into deep wrinkles, the balls (testes) inside increase in size, and the scrotum rises toward the body cavity. Many men report that it is highly exciting when a woman gently and carefully places a part or the whole of the scrotum in the mouth. The best time to do this is after he's well aroused but before orgasm is imminent.

The truly skillful lover keeps constant track of the size and position of her partner's scrotum so that she can exactly gauge his state of arousal and thus prolong or speed up his level of excitement.

The sexual strip. The tender area of skin (called the perineum) that, in men, extends from the anus to the scrotum, and in women extends from the anus to the bottom of the vaginal opening, has tremendous erotic potential. The entire surface is particularly responsive to pressure from the hands and/or mouth. When a firm pressure and stroking is combined with oral sex or manual stimulation of the vagina, penis, or anus, the feelings are especially fabulous.

Least-explored. The anus is probably the least-explored erogenous area and the one with the greatest potential. When I asked men what they felt were the two most erotic areas on the body, all answered "penis, first" and the great majority said "anus, second."

Women too can be highly aroused by anal stimulation, but usually have been so conditioned to think of it as off-limits that we are not aware—or we push aside—the intense erotic feelings that it inspires. Kissing, tonguing, stroking of the anal area and especially the inner rim is a terrific—but too often neglected—turn-on. A gentle, rotating touch at the bud or the entrance of the anus with a well-lubricated finger leads to even more intense sensations. More detail on this kind of pleasuring in an upcoming chapter . . .

CHAPTER 8

September, Italy, continued

IT WAS PAST ELEVEN and the white-aproned waiters had gathered to talk by the open kitchen, a courteous signal that the *ristorante* wanted to close. Diana paid the check and she and Michael strolled back to the hotel.

She wanted to make love again, to hear him gasp with pleasure. His arm was around her, his hand resting on her shoulder. She could feel sexual warmth flowing from even the slightest contact of their bodies: his hand on her back as they moved along the narrow sidewalks turned her into a lightning rod of desire.

Back in their room, Michael used the bathroom as she started to undress. After a minute he came out, a tall white candle burning in each hand.

"Look what I found. They must be for emergencies—or for lovers. This too," he added, displaying a miniature bottle of body lotion.

Using the melting wax, he glued each taper to an ashtray and placed them on the night tables. Slowly and deliberately he clicked off the electric lights and moved over to the bed. He unhooked her bra, slipped the straps down her arms, ran his fingers slowly and languorously over her nipples.

"What lovely breasts you have—I like the way they get so hard and pointy," he said, and leaned over to suckle them. Again she felt a great warmth suffusing the depths of her body. The candlelight flickered on the pale walls, giving off a warm amber light.

He sat on the side of the bed, motionless now, watching her intently. She was filled with desire, but instinctively she knew she should make no move. She was to wait for him.

And slowly, very slowly, every motion graceful and deliberate, he straddled her upper chest, his knees by the sides of her breasts, his legs gripping her hips and thighs. He held his head very high, his back straight as a marble column.

Then he took the body lotion and slowly smoothed

it on his penis as the hot flesh began to rise and the delicate blue veins filled and pulsated. The tip of it was almost above her mouth. Slowly his hands moved back and forth on his swollen penis: it came tantalizingly close to her lips and then swung away.

She felt drugged as she watched the mesmerizing fingers slipping back and forth on his own gleaming, oiled flesh. She opened her mouth, longing to suck his penis into its quivering depths.

But no, he changed the position of his hands. Now his supple sensitive fingers encircled the head of his penis, slowly, slowly squeezing it until a drop appeared at its center. The drop, caught in the candlelight, fell like a diamond onto her neck.

His hands left his erect penis and reached again for the little bottle of lotion. Long, sensuous strokes covered her breasts, her entire torso. Now his buttocks began to lightly skim her chest, the friction from his skin heating her own to a fire. He pressed down harder as he glided back and forth, every move of his body indelibly imprinted on her own. Her breasts burned, the oiled points of her nipples were stinging. As his body burnished hers, his hands began again to move on his penis, faster and faster now, his fingers expertly clasping the swollen, distended, darkened skin when suddenly he threw back his head and gave a low moan, as the hot liquid erupted.

In the small room the shadows played on his body as the light had played on the Michelangelo sculpture they had seen just a few hours before.

"Now," he said, and she could barely hear him, "will you do that for me?"

He knew that she hadn't had an orgasm. Her vagina was congested, contracting, her sexual hunger was boundless. She had never masturbated in front of a man before. She couldn't do it.

Try it, she argued with herself.

I can't, her self responded, I just can't.

He did it for you. Go ahead.

He was lying next to her now, his arm bent at the elbow, head resting on his hand. His smile was gentle, loving.

She reached for the pillows that had scattered and fallen to the floor and piled them up against the heavy mahogany headboard.

"Sit here," she said, patting the pillows to show him how she wanted him to place himself.

Then she walked over to the armoire at the foot of the bed and opened it so that he was reflected, full length, and from differing angles, in both the glass mirrors that hung on the inside of the doors.

Slowly she walked to the other side of the bed and sat down, curving her back along his chest like a cat, the cleft in her buttocks nestling his penis. She placed her legs outside his, leaned her head back, resting it on his shoulder. Their eyes met in the mirror as she reached down slowly to unfurl the soft petal-lips covering her clitoris. With the thumb and forefinger of her left hand, she parted the skin of her vulva, still swollen with desire. Lazily, she dipped the long, slender middle finger of her right hand into the flower-sweet liquid that flowed from deep inside her. She let the finger lie quietly on the clitoris, which had lengthened and become fully erect. Then slowly she flicked her moistened finger over the long, ripe bud a few times and began to circle the satin skin surrounding it.

After a few moments of feathery stroking she felt the mouth of her vagina contract and the deep reserve of anxiety within her melted. She held his eyes in the mirror as she inserted two fingers of her other hand deep into her vagina, never stopping the stroking, rubbing, circling of the most sensitive spot on her body. As she moved her fingers over herself she felt a pressure on the exquisitely sensitive membrane at the edge of her anus. She realized his penis was poised there and the feeling excited her unbearably.

Now, holding her vaginal lips taut, she began quickly, relentlessly, to stroke her clitoris. And now it was beginning to happen, a rising, a dizziness, a bursting, a loss of control as her pelvis moved rhythmically with the endless spasms of climax.

Her body heaved, she caught her breath with gasps and she felt him rise to his knees and fall forward so that she too was on her knees with her hands in front balancing herself on the bed. Sharp, deep thrusts came into her from behind. His hands were on her buttocks, holding them open so that his penis could hurtle down to the deepest parts of her body. Her fingers flew to her glistening nerve-center, hard as a jewel, and she saw herself in the mirror with his magnificent head high above her, in the dancing light of the candles, she saw herself coming and coming and coming . . .

To be continued . . .

CHAPTER 9

Hands On

FOR MANY PEOPLE masturbation is an uncomfortable subject. We know now that it doesn't cause madness or mysterious diseases, but it's something usually done in private and not often discussed. The last few years have radically changed this kind of thinking.

The current point of view is, according to one therapist, that "masturbation is a celebration of yourself, a way of making love to your body. It helps you to become aware of your sensitivities, and your own arousal process. And the more you know about yourself, the more you can transmit that knowledge to your partner so that you get the kind of lovemaking to which you most respond."

People who are happily married and sexually satisfied masturbate. Recent surveys show that a large majority of men and women who rate their relationships as "satisfying" masturbate. One such study showed that 70 percent of young married women and a higher percentage of young married men masturbated. Which simply means that even if you have a lot of sex, you might feel like making love to yourself every so often—or often. But more important than how much you masturbate is *how* and *what* you do, because these are keys to understanding your own body and discovering what turns you on.

Masturbation, say those therapists who regularly prescribe it as part of treatment, can help sensitize and eroticize areas of the body that have been ignored or that previously invoked anxiety. One therapist I interviewed suggested to a patient who was unaware of, or perhaps resisting, total pleasure that he make a thorough exploration of his own body. "One of the first recommendations I made," he said, "was that he begin by breaking a taboo and sticking his finger into his anus."

Most men masturbate with some sort of lubricant such as hand lotion, body lotion, or massage oil. Stimulation is not necessarily limited to the penis. Many men report that the whole genital area is massaged during masturbation, with the anus being almost as sensitive as the penis. Some men will insert a lubricated finger or they will rotate a finger at the opening of the anus to experience a heightened climax.

For several years therapists have been suggesting masturbation—often with the aid of a vibrator—as a way for women to explore their sexuality. Masturbation has also become a primary technique for helping women to reach orgasm or to experience multiple orgasms. But the newest research on female masturbation yields some very interesting information in a related area. It appears that you'll have a better chance to reach orgasm if you make love in a way that corresponds to the one you use to masturbate.

Women masturbate in any number of ways and in a large variety of positions. The following material is a simplified summary of the latest findings on orgasm/masturbation patterns (*Journal of Sex and Marital Therapy*, Summer 1982).

- Women who use their fingers to stimulate the clitoris seem to come to orgasm more easily when a lover also uses his fingers as the main source of stimulation.

- Women who stimulate themselves with water (a strong stream directed at the clitoris) prefer their lovers to give them oral stimulation.

- Women who insert either their fingers or an object

into the vagina while masturbating seem to have orgasm more easily when their partner is giving direct manual stimulation and/or moving his body on hers.

• Women who rub against sheets or other objects as a masturbation pattern have orgasm more frequently when they rub their clitoris directly against their partner when having sex and also when they rub against their partner's thighs or buttocks.

This is interesting and, hopefully, useful information, but there's one important point to remember: Even though a woman will be highly turned on to sex that duplicates the way(s) she masturbates, the most direct trigger to orgasm for almost all women still lies in skillfully using your hands/mouth/tongue as stimulants.

One further suggestion that I heard from several therapists: Don't always stick to your usual masturbation technique. If you usually masturbate while lying on your back or pressing your legs together, try stimulating yourself in other positions and in other ways. For example, you can insert a vibrator into the vagina if you've never done so before, or you can explore yourself anally with a well-lubricated finger. (Don't insert this same finger into the vagina without washing it first. Bacteria in the anus can cause problems in the vaginal tract.)

Today, masturbation is considered one of the best ways of discovering what turns you on. Lots of us still suffer from hang-ups about our bodies. The surest way to get over the common anxiety that your natural body odors are a turn-off is to taste your own vaginal secretions during masturbation. Another area that causes anxiety is anal contact. Many women feel that there is something embarrassing or degrading about anal arousal, and they've put it off-limits. You might discover some interesting erotic information about yourself if you investigate this area on your own. Exploring your body in new ways helps you give yourself permission to be sensual and sexual as well as learning what it is, specifically, that feels *great* to you.

"A Special Kind of Togetherness"

These days mutual masturbation is also commonly recommended as part of sex therapy for couples because it helps to show each lover the kind of stimulation and timing sequence that feels best.

Not only do you give/get a clear picture of what your lover likes, but the turn-on benefits of masturbating in your lover's presence can be terrific. One man, who was seeing a sexual therapist with his wife, sketched his first experience with mutual masturbation: "I just didn't want to do it in front of her, and she didn't want to do it either, but we wanted to give the therapy a real chance for success. I bit the bullet and went first. She was so turned on that she started to masturbate herself. It was a real breakthrough for us sexually."

Some men and women are reluctant to masturbate unless they are in a totally private place, but the number of women who have masturbated in a partner's presence in one study was shown to be over 50 percent. As any therapist or marriage counselor will tell you, much information is transmitted to a lover during masturbation. But perhaps, ultimately, the turn-on benefits are the real kick. "When I'm doing it to myself," explains a twenty-five-year-old paralegal from San Diego, California, "it's like I'm sending my own electrical waves through the air. My boyfriend picks up those vibrations, and it turns him on in a way nothing else can do. For us it's a special kind of togetherness."

CHAPTER 10

The Point of No Return

WHEN I BEGAN the research on *Great Sex,* I thought I'd find very little that could possibly be enlightening on the subject of orgasm. From the oceans of books and articles that confronted me in the library it seemed quite clear that everything had been explained many times before. Although at times I found myself drowning in the technical depths of orgasmic detail, I discovered that the most recent research yields some very interesting information for both men and women. So there *is* more to know—and, amazingly, even more to enjoy.

The Multiples Mania

After Masters and Johnson confirmed that the female of the species could have more than one orgasm, all hell broke loose in American bedrooms. The "capacity for" was translated by many to mean "obligation to," and a wild scramble to experience the divine multiplicity of superpleasure began. The new emphasis was on peak performance, and it put the pressure on men and women alike. Men worried about whether they could give their mates multiple orgasms, and women began to fake more than ever in order not to disappoint their hardworking partners. "I would lie in bed and think, I'm taking too long; he's getting bored by now; at this rate I'll never even come once," was how one woman described the anxiety she felt.

Finally we're seeing a backlash to all the hoopla about orgasm. Up to now, the assumption has been that orgasm is the main source of satisfaction for women. Recent studies show precisely the reverse: *satisfaction,* not orgasm(s), is what counts with most women. There are other, important kinds of satisfaction that women get from lovemaking besides orgasm—intimacy, physical closeness, tenderness, affection, to name a few. Further, it's been shown that if a woman considers orgasm an important part of lovemaking, it's likely that she *will* experience an orgasm because she herself will create the conditions (and the stimulation) that lead to it.

All this means is that there's a healthy new attitude around: If a woman has an orgasm, fine; if not, fine too. The eighties' view is that *more is not necessarily better* and that each of us is responsible for our own self when it comes to having good/great sex.

How, where, and *why* a woman has an orgasm (if and when she wants it) has also been subjected to intense scrutiny, and here is the most up-to-date information available.

It's currently thought that 10 percent of women cannot have orgasm and that another 10 percent can have orgasm through fantasy alone. Most of us are somewhere in between. It's still not clear if a woman who can have one orgasm can have multiples. If a woman has not ever had an orgasm, the chances are very good that she will experience one through masturbation and/or the use of a vibrator. Ditto for multiple orgasms: The strategy is to have one orgasm and just keep going with the vibrator to see if you can have another—and another. If you've tried these techniques and are still what is known as anorgasmic (meaning no orgasms at all), or haven't experienced multiples and you'd like to, several therapy sessions with a qualified sex counselor might be the answer.

If you've had problems with orgasm, you're not alone— it's been estimated that *75 percent of women have difficulty in experiencing orgasm and approximately*

*one out of every two women does not have orgasm during
sexual relations.* In fact, the majority of us have
orgasm(s) outside of intercourse, usually during manual stimulation of the clitoris.

After years of haggling about vaginal versus clitoral
orgasms, it seems pretty clear that there *are* two kinds
of orgasms, possibly three. The first comes from stimulation of the clitoris, the second comes from stimulation of a certain area or areas (X zones) within the
vagina, and the third type of orgasm, which many
experts still question, is considered to be a blending of
the vaginal and clitoral. As to whether there is such a
thing as female ejaculation, the evidence is still largely
inconclusive.

A myth that still persists: that a woman should have
orgasm during intercourse—preferably during her
partner's thrusting. If you'd like to have an orgasm,
the *least efficient* way is to try to achieve it by joining
with your partner's thrusting. The direct route to the
most common kind of orgasm—for most women—is
sustained stimulation of the clitoris. Vaginal orgasms
can be induced manually or with thrusting from certain positions. More about this on page 116.

Men and Multiples

As any man knows only too well, an erection is not
under his control. (You can, by the way, have an
orgasm/ejaculation without an erection.) But what

many men aren't as aware of is the fact that although erections are not a matter of will, ejaculation *can* be controlled—and this is one of the routes to terrific sex. Several men I interviewed had experienced "multiple orgasms," and their descriptions matched those in recent scientific studies.

"Some men have the ability to time their ejaculation down to the actual thrust," explained one MD. "This kind of refined awareness takes time, and acute sensitivity to the threshold of ejaculation, but it is possible. Learning to accurately anticipate that point is basically a matter of experience. You know that you're going to come. If you stop everything and simmer down, you won't have an ejaculation. Each man differs, but in about thirty seconds you can start again and continue until you decide to stop a second time or to have ejaculation." You can try developing this skill with a partner or you can experiment on your own during masturbation.

The highroad to multiple orgasms lies in pinpointing the moment when ejaculation is imminent (this feeling has been described as being akin to the start of a sneeze!). At that moment—when you feel you're going over the threshold—the thrusting or stimulation is stopped and a mild, involuntary mini-orgasm will occur without ejaculation. When thrusting or manual/oral stimulation is resumed, you will come to another threshold and another low-powered orgasm. You can stop thrusting and begin again or go on to full orgasm—with ejaculation. The stopping and resuming of stimulation can be repeated several times— the men I spoke to said three or four mini-orgasms was about their limit—but one formal study recorded a man who reported ten! A final orgasm (after one or multiple mini-orgasms) was, not surprisingly, considered "indescribably intense."

Much has been written about the PC muscle for women. This interior muscle can be strengthened and used for gripping the penis, and may be useful in heightening a woman's orgasm, although this attribute is still open to question. (The exercise, developed by a gynecologist named Kegel, consists simply in tightening and relaxing the same muscle that is used in stopping and starting the flow of urine.)

I had never heard of a male PC until I started the research for this book. Indeed, men do anatomically have a PC muscle, but according to one eminent UCLA physician I interviewed, it does not appear to be useful sexually.

However, I found a provocative reference to the male PC in an article by Donna Powell entitled "The Ultimate Male Orgasm" (*Sexology Today,* November 1981) and reprinted in a widely read text-book/journal, *Human Sexuality 84/85.*

"The male who possesses a really powerful PC," writes the author after consultation with sex researcher William Hartman, PhD, "can maintain a firm erection for hours and can enjoy more ecstatic orgasms during one sex episode than most men enjoy in a month." In case you're interested, these are the two exercises Powell describes.

Each time you urinate, stop the flow forcefully at least six times. "Persist," says the author, "and your PC will have no choice but to get stronger. (And so will your orgasm.)"

A second exercise, called a Kegel, she explains, "consists of consciously tightening the anal sphincter (rectum) and the muscles at the base of the penis. When you do a correct Kegel your penis will move slightly. You are also doing Kegels when you have an erection and you tighten to make your penis move up and down." Fifty to one hundred or even up to three hundred Kegels per day are recommended over a period of two months.

Prostate Orgasms

When a man is sexually excited, the prostate gland, a walnut-sized mass that can be stimulated through the anus, swells and hardens—it is erectile tissue like the penis. If the prostate is stimulated or massaged in tandem with stimulation of his penis, a man will usually have a wild, knock-out orgasm. Men who have experienced so-called prostate orgasms describe them as "deeper," "incredibly intense," "out of this world." More on how to have an internal or an external prostate orgasm in Chapter 12.

CHAPTER 11

Ultimate Sex

*Good sex is when everything is working and
you're both feeling good . . .
Great sex is a road to the soul.*
        F.E.D., New York City

THE INFORMATION in this chapter describes
what great, knock-out sex is all about—*physically.* This
is the refined, sophisticated stuff that the best, most
knowledgeable lovers use to send a body to the sexual
summit. The ideas, information, and techniques here
are simple to learn—*using* them is another matter.
You have to give yourself permission to be open to
physical pleasures that might at first sound too exotic

or even upsetting. It's up to you to decide how much or how far is right for you. If you're uncomfortable with something, don't do it because you feel obligated to or you feel it is your duty, but at least keep in mind that cautiously experimenting with something new might lead you into a wonderfully delicious unknown.

A young, extremely attractive, obviously sensual doctor summed it up when he said in his direct way, "Someone who doesn't know is not as bad as someone who is unwilling."

Knowing what buttons to press, what moves to make, will lead you to technically proficient sex (which has its value!), but to have Great Sex, you need the physical know-how plus affection, caring, warmth—and, more than anything, love.

What It Takes to Have Great, Loving Sex

Just as there are great cooks, great basketball players, great writers, there are great lovers. After you've interviewed several hundred people, you begin to get a feeling about who's good in bed, who's so-so, and who's outright fabulous. You can't necessarily tell from what they say or how well they say it. Some people just seem to communicate an intuitive understanding and delight in what sensuality and sexuality is all about. Interestingly, these men and women all repeated the same key ideas.

The "secret" of great sex lies in concentrating on your

own excitement and then your lover's—or vice versa. The idea is that you alternate in giving the ultimate pleasure to your lover and then actively seek the ultimate pleasure for yourself.

This sounds very obvious, but many people don't put this idea into practice because what it means is that you *both* must take turns being active and passive. This is easier said than done. Many women are reluctant to take the lead ("what will he think of me; will he be threatened?") and many men are anxious with the idea of being "passive" ("I should be *doing* something").

Most women are comfortable in the age-old role of giving pleasure, but *actively* seeking it for ourselves is something new. The opposite holds true for many men: they know how to get pleasure for themselves, but it's new for them to simply *be available* and enjoy seeing a woman take her pleasure.

Great lovers aren't confined by roles such as "man is the sex expert" and "the woman takes his lead." Many if not most of us have been brought up with this kind of thinking, and changing the way we feel about sex is not the easiest thing in the world. But it's definitely worth trying. You can begin just by being flexible and not always sticking to specified ways of doing things. If you find yourself uncomfortable about attempting something new or unpredictable, take it one small step at a time—and try not to close your mind to it unless you're really sure it's definitely not for you.

"Be aware of your lover's level of arousal at all times,"

counsels a highly sensual architect from Southampton, New York. Devoted sensualists all concur. The reason this is so important is that it gives you a guideline as to how much to intensify or decrease stimulation. By knowing fairly precisely when your partner is near orgasm, for example, you have several options. You might want to stop what you're doing for a moment and begin something else so that you build up to a higher and higher climax. Or you might want to heighten the moment by adding anal/manual stimulation. A great lover, as described by a man with a reputation for being one, "is someone who knows the repertoire of pleasurable things and who's quick enough to sense that it's time to vary what you're doing and go on to something different." This sense of perfect sexual pitch comes from closely watching your lover for the signs that show his or her degree of arousal.

You can generally tell a woman's level of arousal by certain physical changes. Not all women experience these, but here are some common signs: The nipples become erect, the breasts may harden, the vagina is well-lubricated, there is clitoral erection, a deepening or brightening of the rose color of the lips of the vagina as well as the interior areas, a pink "sex flush" across the chest, and tightening of the buttocks, legs, and toes—all these are signs along the path that leads to orgasm.

For men the most common physical signs of arousal are: semierection or erection, followed by changes in the scrotum. As the scrotum begins to wrinkle and ascend toward the body, orgasm is near. Some men may experience nipple erection, sex flush across the chest, and tightening of buttocks, legs, and a few drops of pre-ejaculatory fluid.

Watching your partner's physical reactions very closely—as well as listening to his or her sighs, moans, whispers, and words—is the best way you can develop the sense of timing that's a hallmark of the sensitive, sensational lover.

One last thought to keep in mind: To most people the act of intercourse—the time when a man's penis is in a woman's vagina—is *the* real thing, the essential ingredient in sex. Don't limit yourself when you think about sex; throw out the old, hackneyed compartments of Foreplay, Real Thing (penis-in-vagina), and Afterplay. Instead, remember that there's all kinds of great sex besides intercourse: genital sex, oral sex, manual sex, anal sex, and all sorts of wonderful permutations and combinations of the above. That's what the rest of this chapter is all about.

The Oral Majority

Just what is it about oral sex that makes it such a big deal? Why is it so important to men? Why is it so problematic to many women? Oral sex has gone from taboo to obligatory. What was once forbidden is now commonplace, yet in *every interview* I've done, the subject has come up with a certain amount of anxiety attached to it.

Oral sex is important to men for several reasons. The first is that it *just plain feels great* (when it's done skillfully). A second is emotional: Oral sex confirms that a woman enjoys that part of a man's body which is most important to him. "It's the very deepest way that a woman can acknowledge my maleness," said a computer programmer from Chicago.

Men who perform and receive oral sex, according to the Blumstein-Schwartz landmark study (*American Couples: Money, Work, and Sex,* Morrow, 1984), say they are happier, more satisfied, than those who do not. Many men rate oral sex as the most intimate kind, and the majority of men I've interviewed complain that they are not getting as much oral sex as they want, or that women don't really know how to do it or, if they do know, they don't seem to be willing to do it enough.

Women, on the other hand, talk about oral sex in a different way. Often they do it from a sense of duty, or to be considered good in bed, or because they are afraid of losing their lover if they don't please him. Some women are fearful that they may gag, or taste urine, or have to swallow ejaculate. If a man is giving oral sex to his lover, she may worry about the natural odors of her body, or she may feel that he really doesn't like doing it but thinks he must.

Many women have said that they want more, or better, oral sex but they're afraid to bring up the subject. "If he doesn't do it, you naturally assume he doesn't *want* to," says a New York sportswear designer. "It's a very uncomfortable thing to have to ask a man to do something you suspect he's not dying to do." More on how to deal with this in Chapter 15.

"The Best Oral Sex I Ever Had . . ."

I interviewed a very sexually sophisticated New York man who told me that he had a lover who had given him the best oral sex he'd ever had—and he'd had a lot. He thought she might consent to being interviewed. I finally reached her by phone in San Francisco and asked her what she was doing that was so special.

"First of all, I *love* doing it," she explained. "I love to be able to really turn a man on—to blow his mind as well as his penis. A lot of men have told me they think most women are doing it to them as a favor or to show how much they know—that's a turn-off. The real secret has to do with *time*. I always feel I have all the time in the world—and I let a man know it by going slow, feeling completely unhurried. I start out with the shaft, because the feeling is less intense there. Then I work around the balls and back to the shaft, keeping the head in reserve because that's the place that has the most feeling. I like to spend a long, long time working up to the head; it's a form of teasing really. Finally I get there and take it all in my mouth . . ."

Even over the long-distance telephone lines you could tell that Janice genuinely enjoys sex, and the feeling is a tremendous turn-on. One of the best ways to show how much you're enjoying your lover is, as Jan described, to take your time in making love. There's almost nothing more unappealing than someone who's hurrying everything along.

I asked Jan if there were any special tips that she could pass on. "I think I've tried everything. I've sucked ice before I've sucked a penis. I've heated my mouth with hot cider, and I've even rinsed out with Chloraseptic mouthwash, which numbs and stimulates at the same time. I've been told the feelings are fleeting but fun. I've tried whipped cream and warm fudge sauce and even honey—which is, by the way, too sticky for my taste—but there are really no tips that make oral sex any better than it could possibly be if you have sensitive hands and a willing mouth."

Perhaps the biggest secret to expert oral sex for both men and women is mental: *Concentrate* on pleasuring your lover. If you start thinking of the dishes in the kitchen sink, or the bills to be paid, your lover will sense it immediately and you will be cheating both of you out of something wonderful.

There's one other thing to keep in mind when it comes to oral sex: All motions should be done *continuously.* You wouldn't want him to stop stroking you on the clitoris when you're intensely stimulated— so be just as considerate of him.

Step-by-Step

In my two previous books I wrote on oral sex step-by-step for both men and women. I'll outline the basic points again briefly—you'll need to know these before you go on to the really knock-out stuff.

This is what women need to know: Each man likes a different touch and may respond to different kinds of stimulation. One of the best things you can do is ask your husband or lover to guide your head and/or your mouth with his own hands so you get the rhythm and stroking feeling he prefers. If you're shy and simply can't talk about it (yet), the guideline to keep in mind is that most men like a firm touch on the shaft of the penis ("The kind of pressure you get from a hearty handshake," said one man) and a lighter touch on the scrotum.

Now, think of your mouth as the opening of a vagina and think of your hands as an extension of your mouth. What you're aiming for is to duplicate the feeling a man has when he's inside you. But there's an important difference. You have far more control over your mouth and hands than you do over your vagina, so you can give an even broader range of exquisite sensations.

Begin by making your tongue sharp and pointed, and use it to probe gently around the scrotum, shaft, and, very lightly, the head. Begin to lick and stroke the penis, concentrating on the ridge that runs down the center of the underside. Go slowly and sensuously. Lightly flick your tongue back and forth on the little ridge of skin where the head is joined to the shaft—an area of maximum sensation.

Relax, remember to breathe, and improvise a bit. You may want to lick or kiss his penis or stroke it slowly lengthwise with your tongue. Return to where the head and shaft connect. *Take your time.* Make smooth, fluid movements. Now envelop his penis with your mouth. Your mouth should be wide open, the lips drawn back as far as possible in a tight oval covering your teeth, his penis on your tongue. If you're having any mental problems about what you're doing, concentrate completely on your physical actions.

Now begin the oral friction in which your mouth and tongue imitate the reciprocal moving and kneading action of the vagina. Move your mouth back and forth, up and down, on the penis, constantly keeping in mind that your lips and tongue should feel like a very snug vagina. Begin slowly and increase your speed subtly at every forward stroke.

Some men prefer having as much of the penis in the mouth as possible. Others feel that the mouth need cover only the head, the most sensitive area, plus one or two inches down the shaft. If your husband or lover falls into this latter category, then use one of your hands as an extension of your mouth. Make a snug circle around the penis with your thumb and forefinger; the rest of your hand is clasping the shaft. Keep your mouth in contact with your thumb and forefinger. Now move your hand up and down the penis in the same rhythm as your mouth. As your mouth goes down onto the shaft, your hand goes downward too, and vice versa.

You'll need some sort of lotion to replicate the vagina's own lubrication so that your hand motions are fluid and slippery/sensuous. Most men say that saliva dries out too fast—a *nontasting* body lotion or unflavored lotions found in health food stores is recommended. Even with these, however, there is a tendency to medicinal taste. The problem is usually solved by applying lubricant (warm it in your hands first) to the lower shaft of the penis, the part in contact with your hand.

If your man likes to put as much of his penis in your mouth as he can, you may prefer to stick with saliva as a lubricant unless he prefers something else. If he wants to thrust while in your mouth, you may have a tendency to gag. If it happens, don't be upset. Take a second's pause, a deep breath to relax your throat muscles, and keep on going. Experience exercises the upper throat and helps eliminate gagging.

Oral stimulation is wildly intense for most men. Take it wickedly slow and easy at first and then build up the intensity by increasing your up-and-down speed. You can sense when an orgasm is imminent because the skin of the scrotum starts wrinkling and the entire scrotum begins to ascend toward the body cavity. At this point you can ease up on the stimulation, stop it entirely, and start again in half a minute or so—or you can go on to something different. If, however, you both wish to go on to climax, you face the question of swallowing the man's ejaculate. Don't do anything that you're uncomfortable with. Some men consider it a very special love-sign if a woman swallows their sperm. Others feel it's not that big a deal. It's basically a matter of whether or not *you* feel comfortable with what you're doing.

Men also have a good deal to learn about satisfying a woman orally. Many women still believe that their lovers are uncomfortable with oral sex—a good number of men whom I interviewed acknowledged this. The first problem area for a man is knowing what to do and when to do it. "Things change so fast with a woman," commented one man. "I found it was almost impossible to gauge just what kind of touch and rhythm was right, so now I just ask: 'How does this feel?' or 'Tell me when you want me to go faster or slower.'" If you keep in mind that a woman is not as genitally oriented as a man, meaning that she likes to be sexually aroused through kissing and hugging as well as direct erogenous contact, you'll be off on the right track. And most women would be delighted to hear "I love doing this with you" if that's what you honestly feel.

Many women are concerned that the vaginal area—particularly natural body secretions—might be distasteful. The vagina, like the eye, is self-cleaning, and there is no reason that with normal hygiene, its natural scent should cause any offense. However, if either of you has any trouble with this, the simple and obvious solution is to take a bath or shower. If she uses a diaphragm, you might want to incorporate it into lovemaking by inserting it later so that you can avoid the medicinal taste of spermicidal jelly.

First think of your tongue and hands as being able to give the most marvelous range of sensations to your wife or lover. Remember that with your tongue and hands you have the control and the capacity to give her the most intense kind of stimulation. Always remember that all your motions should be done continuously unless your lover requests otherwise. Unlike a man's, a woman's level of arousal falls off steeply if stimulation is stopped even for a second or two. Many women respond quickly to oral/manual stimulation, but some need as much as ten to fifteen minutes—or more—to build up to a high peak. Many women have said that they worry about taking too long. You can help your lover relax and reassure her by an unhurried, I-have-all-the-time-in-the-world attitude.

You can use your tongue in many ways. Keep it pointed, then make it rounded or flat. A gentle to lightly firm pressure is a good way to begin. Concentrate at first on the areas outside the clitoris, going from the outer lips of the vagina to the shaft of the clitoris and then, finally, to the clitoris itself unless you are signaled to stop. (Some women can take very little direct stimulation.)

Begin by kissing and stroking the outer lips with your pointed tongue. *Go slowly and take your time.* Gently explore the area, going from top to bottom on each of the lips. Then, holding the lips open, begin to stroke the bottom of the shaft of the clitoris. You'll need a pointed tongue to do this best, as the clitoris is short. Go back and forth, circle around it, not touching the glans or the head. Relax, don't hurry, let her know by eye contact that you enjoy doing this. You can also use one of your hands to stimulate her breasts and the other to aid you in further arousing her genitally.

Apply only *slightly* more pressure as you feel a higher degree of arousal. Do not worry if the clitoris is not yet erect; remember that a woman's rate of arousal is much slower than yours. If at any time you begin to feel anxious, simply concentrate on your breathing and your tongue movements and *don't* stop what you're doing unless she wants you to.

As her level of arousal builds, you might switch to manually stimulating the clitoris, keeping your finger pressure light and sensitive. At the same time you could explore the opening of the vagina with your pointed tongue. Keep in mind that if your stimulation of the clitoris is too heavy-handed or your movements become mechanical or too repetitive (for example, you continually stroke from left to right), the clitoris may become numb.

After a certain amount of stimulation you may feel you've "lost" the clitoris. What has happened is that it has retracted under its "hood," a natural response when a woman is highly stimulated or orgasm is about to occur. Continue your movements until orgasm.

Unless she requests you to stop, go on stimulating her until she has another orgasm or switch to some other area of pleasure.

Those are the basics—now you can go on to the exquisite refinements—and from *there* into the outer limits . . .

CHAPTER 12

Taboo and Terrific

CERTAIN COMBINATIONS of physical stimulation can result in double-whammy, super-fantastic sensations. This is where skill plays a major part: You have to know what you're doing and when to do it. Once again keep in mind that some of the material here may strike you as too far-out or even taboo. But in great sex the only taboos are the ones you set yourself.

Here is the step-by-step information you'll need.

Knockouts—for Men

For most men the prostate gland is as sensitive (some men say even more sensitive) as the head of the penis. A man's prostate is located about two or three inches up the rectum. It lies toward the belly and is about the size of a walnut. Applying pressure to the prostate during oral sex gives an incredibly intense sensation.

You can stimulate the prostate either internally or externally.

External prostate stimulation. Touch under the scrotum (during an erection) and you'll feel a hard rod, which is the extension of the penis. You can trace this rod right up to the anus. During oral sex, as your mouth moves up and down on your lover's penis, one hand applies *firm* pressure at a point a half inch or so down from the opening of the anus. You can use the heel of your hand or your index and next finger together. Apply this firm pressure for a second or two, then ease up. When you see that orgasm is imminent (the testes are beginning to ascend) apply an even firmer pressure nonstop until orgasm.

Some men say the sensation is heightened *even more* with this technique: While your mouth is moving up and down on the penis, take your thumb and forefinger and encircle the top of the scrotum, making sure that the testicles are beneath the snug ring of your fingers. Hold your thumb and forefinger together while you apply either the back of the hand or the heel of this same hand to the root of the penis, about a half-inch down from the anus. Your pressure must be quite firm so that the root of the penis will be pressed against the prostate for maximum feeling.

Taboo and terrific. The anus has a long history of taboos, but anal pleasure for a man in combination with oral stimulation can be truly knock-out sex. A young New York physician gave me this precise information on how to stimulate the prostate internally.

First, your nails must be very short. Anything that extends over the fleshy part of your finger means that your nails are too long. Lubricate your index or third finger with a good body cream. KY jelly or Vaseline are not recommended: use something that is hypoallergenic and/or contains vitamin E. (Vitamin E is thought to heal any minor abrasions that might be on the anal membrane.)

Touch the anal verge (rim) and you'll feel an initial contraction, which is a normal reflex. This reflex is followed by relaxation. At that point begin to insert your finger gently and *very* gradually. You may feel another contraction and then relaxation. Insert your finger up to about the second knuckle during the relaxation time. (You don't want to force your finger through a contraction, because it's obviously antipleasurable.) You should feel a hard lump the size of a walnut, lying toward the belly: this is the prostate gland. Apply a light pressure with the pad of your finger or, if he can take it, rotate the finger *lightly* no more than an eighth or quarter of an inch. This should be done in combination with direct stimulation of the penis. If orgasm happens, which is the case for the majority of men, you will be able to feel the contractions of the prostate. Remember, all of your movements should be done fluidly and *very* slowly. "Limit your movements," cautions Dr. B.G. "No man wants to feel a finger flailing around there."

Head down. This erotic high was described to me by a young, athletic medical student from Los Angeles. "Do this only if you're agile and *in good health* and have no problems with your breathing or your back," he cautions.

Here is the how-to: When, during oral sex, a climax is imminent, your lover lies crosswise on the bed, knees open and bent. He is on his back, his head and shoulders off the edge of the bed toward the floor, his arms arched back with hands on the floor—elbows bent or straight, whichever he prefers. Tuck a pillow under his shoulders or the small of his back for extra comfort.

"You can describe it as a half handstand," is the way the medical student put it. "Most of your weight is on your hands, and the edge of the bed is the fulcrum for the top part of the body. Her head is between your legs and her shoulders are supporting your legs. Or you can place your legs outside her arms and shoulders. As you come to a climax, the combination of the reverse blood flow (toward the head) and the physical contractions you feel will give you an *incredibly heightened orgasm.*" Stay in the same position until the orgasmic contractions subside and then *very slowly* lift your head until you are in a sitting position. You may feel quite dizzy, but the feeling will pass in a few seconds.

The same "handstand position" applies to women during oral sex, but the feelings can be even more intense. Since a man usually has more strength, he can kneel on his knees and totally support the lower part of her body by placing her legs over his shoulders. His mouth has direct contact with her clitoris while her hands are on the floor. Since there is obviously a great flow of blood to the head in this upside down position, it should be held for only a *few* seconds and should be done *only* if both of you are physically very fit.

Ultimate Sensations—for Women

A wonderful range and variety of ultimate sensations is available to women. Here's the step-by-step information you'll need.

The tandem. Hands must be scrupulously clean and fingernails trimmed very short. The second and third fingers should be well lubricated with body cream, lotion, or KY jelly. Now, begin to slowly and gently insert one or both fingers into the vagina. Reach above the pubic bone and apply somewhat firmer pressure, moving minutely until you find the area of maximum response. (In most women it will be on the vaginal wall toward the belly, but in others it may be on the wall toward her back.) As you are doing this you might want to continue stimulating her orally.

You can also add anal stimulation if she's interested in it. Here's how: Use your other hand, with the index or third finger very well lubricated. Insert your finger into the anus as described before—during the moment of relaxation following the initial contraction. Once inserted, you should be able to feel your other finger stimulating the vaginal walls. Move the two fingers (the one in the vagina and the one in the anus) in tandem, making *slow, very small* massagelike movements. Then move your fingers, again slowly and extremely gently, in tiny in-and-out movements. You can use your thumb to continue stimulating the clitoris.

At the risk of sounding repetitive, it's important to remember that all your stroking, massaging, rubbing should be done fluidly, sensually, rhythmically—and lightly.

Incredible vibrations. If you're not interested in internal anal stimulation, another extremely powerful range of sensations can be had by using a vibrator. You can manually continue to palpate (or stimulate/massage) the erotically sensitive X zone deep in the interior of the vagina while applying the vibrator to the clitoris.

A variation on this: Lubricate the tip of a penis-shaped vibrator and rotate it at the rim of the anus. During this your finger(s) can still be in the vagina, and you could also be orally stroking or kissing the clitoris. This has the effect of a triple whammy.

Again, don't forget that although what has been described here has focused on the genital/anal areas, the breasts are also maximum-sensation areas for most women, so you might for example want to combine vaginal stimulation with gentle rolling or massaging of the nipples. And kissing, of course, is always most welcome.

Counterpressures. One of the absolute heights of sensation for women who have an X zone on the front wall of the vagina is to combine the firm interior rhythmic stroking with a hand that is pressed firmly on the exterior of the lower abdomen, just above the pubic bone. These counterpressures can "blow you away, they're so fantastic" says one woman.

Newfangled spanking. This modern variation of an old-school theme applies to both men and women. As your level of arousal rises, you might want to try this version of "spanking." Bring all your fingers together as if you were trying to fashion a small dome. Use this cupped hand to lightly spank your lover. First places to try: the upper back, small of the back. Then: the buttocks, the tops of the inner thighs, and, *very lightly*, the area below the mons pubis so that the heel of your hand is *very lightly* in contact with the clitoris.

If you're trying this technique on a man, the best time is just before a climax. Stop whatever you've been doing that has put him on the brink and gently spank the strip under the scrotum and over the anus.

It's a wise idea to have tried out beforehand the amount of pressure that feels best to him.

The slight suction that comes from your cupped hand is what makes the sensation so terrific. Obviously, if you're spanking the buttocks, you can use a firmer touch than you would with the genitals. The key to pleasure here is sensitive experimentation to see what degree of firmness is right for different parts of the body.

Sequence

All of the techniques described above can give exquisitely interesting sensations, but if you use them inappropriately you're going to be disappointed. For instance, if you stripped off your clothes, kissed a couple of times, and went right into spanking, the chances are that it would feel odd, out-of-sync. And that's because there's a natural sequence to lovemaking. What this means is simply that you must create and be aware of a buildup/slowdown flow—you must, in short, develop a sense of timing.

The techniques described in this chapter should be used only after you're really turned on to each other, when you're trying to heighten and intensify every feeling. You don't *start* with deep vaginal exploration, or anal or prostate stimulation: you lead up to these through warmth, affection, kissing, manual and oral arousal.

If you don't have a natural sense of sequence, all it takes is a little practice. Just keep in mind that the basic idea is a slow but steady buildup/falloff/buildup of sensation.

Positions

I've described some variations on oral sex that can bring on fantastic orgasms. But although oral/manual sex can stimulate exciting physical feeling, most men and women agree that the emotional impact of penis-in-vagina sex is ultimately most fulfilling, most intimate.

Innumerable sexual positions have been lyrically or clinically described by every sex writer since Ovid. You can have sex standing up, sitting down, lying down, half-lying/half-standing—anytime, anyplace and anything you can conceive of is possible. Unfortunately many people ignore this kind of imaginative variation. One of the insidious ways to slip into the bedroom-boredom syndrome is to stick to one or two positions. You don't have to try for some sort of sexual version of the decathlon, but indulging in novelty can have some exhilarating effects. Here are some ideas about which positions work best.

Generally speaking, men feel the most sensation and the most pleasure in those positions where the penis is *most snugly* fitted into the vagina. Women feel maximum stimulation in those positions where the friction on the clitoris and its surrounds is greatest, and where the penis moves rhythmically against the X zone inside the vagina.

The missionary position is, of course, the great American favorite. For men it feels especially terrific when a woman raises her legs in order to allow deeper penetration. The knee-chest position, when she has her knees pressed to her chest with her legs extended beyond his shoulders, is usually the position in which the vagina is most extended and elongated. Thus the penis fits snugly and penetration is much deeper. With this deeper penetration comes benefits for women: more intense friction on the vaginal/clitoral area and a literal feeling of fullness and satisfaction.

A man has a better chance of extending the time of his erection in the woman-on-top position. Sensation is not as intense because his thrusting is not as deep and direct and the woman is more in control of movement. Some women say they are uncomfortable about being on top because a man may feel threatened. The great majority of men I interviewed said they enjoyed sex with their partners astride them because it gave them a chance to lie back and enjoy without having to be responsible for all the movements.

The side-by-side position is favored by Masters and Johnson because it is democratic and there's equal freedom of movement. But it's not terrific for penetration, and, precisely because it's so egalitarian, men and women don't list it as a favorite.

It's interesting to note that in the fifties, when Alfred Kinsey did his pioneering research on the sex lives of Americans, he found that only one in ten married couples had ever used any form of what is called the rear-entry (or, unfortunately "doggy-style") position. In contrast, last year's widely quoted *Playboy* survey found that almost half of the married couples had tried some version of it, and about a fifth of couples under twenty-five used it often.

The possibilities for incredibly intense pleasure are manifold in variations of this position because of the access to the vagina's X zone(s). The vagina slants toward the small of the back: thus a rear-entry position in which the penis thrusts into the forward wall can be wildly stimulating for a woman.

Similar intensity is possible when a woman is astride a man, sitting almost straight up on him. You can also experience particularly pleasurable deep-vaginal stimulation when he is sitting on a straightback chair and you lower your body onto his lap. You can either face him or have your back to his chest—whichever is the closest anatomical fit.

Perhaps the best guidelines to keep in mind about positions are these:

• Don't stick to the same one or two all the time.

• Positions that allow for deep thrusting and snugness (which can be accomplished by varying the closeness and placement of the woman's legs) feel absolutely great to men: man on top with woman in knee-chest position, rear entry in any of its variations, the X position (face to foot with woman on top and each partner between the other's legs).

- Positions that put you at right angles with each other (woman sitting straight on top, woman lying on bed facing him with her feet thrown over his shoulders, and rear entry) give maximum interior sensation to her because the penis is thrust into the front vaginal wall.

- Each couple is constructed differently. You both must find those positions that give the most amount of penetration and friction. Trial and error is the best—and most delightful—method of discovery.

Note: If you've had anal sex, don't switch to vaginal insertion without first washing the penis. Bacteria from the anus can easily cause problems inside the vagina.

The Cliché Climax

The notion that simultaneous orgasm is the ne plus ultra of sex seems to have been part of the fallout from the sexual revolution. The view today is that attempts at mutual orgasm may actually deprive a couple of pleasure.

"It's not something that we strive for," says a

twenty-nine-year-old Philadelphia teacher. "I want to enjoy his climax, see and feel what it's like for him when he's going over the top. And I want him to enjoy my orgasm in the same way. If we're both having an orgasm, we're concentrating on ourselves and we miss out on each other's pleasure."

Obviously there's room for all kinds of orgasms—single, serial, extended, mutual—the choice of pleasure is, as always, up to you.

The Elite Lover

Many people see sex solely as a buildup of physical stimulation ending in climax and, hopefully, some afterglow. The great lover views things quite differently. This description comes from a man known to be a really great lover.

"There's three kinds of stimulation: mental, emotional, and physical. You want to turn someone on at every one of these levels. I find that the best kind of sex for me is not a straight upward climb toward climax, but when periods of pure sexual play are alternated with closeness and caring. We'll build up to a first high point and then break to talk and kiss for a while, keeping the physical at a low hum by slow stroking or touching. Then we're off again, building up even higher with oral sex or whatever. We deliberately stop at a point where one or both of us is dying for more, more, more. After that, we just keep on going to a place that I can't describe—outer space, I guess."

And that's one of the most accurate descriptions about what great lovers do that I've come across so far.

The Odds on Having Great Sex

Great lovers are also aware of the realities of lovemaking. You're not going to have what I've called summit sex every time or even most of the time. Psychologist Barry W. McCarthy, PhD (in *Journal of Sex and Marital Therapy*, Summer 1984) gives these odds:

- It is normal for about 5 to 10 percent of sexual experiences to be unpleasant.

- 10 percent of sexual experiences will be mediocre.

- 15 percent of the time one lover will find it good and the other will go along because he/she enjoys the lover's pleasure.

- 25 percent of the time both lovers will enjoy sex, but one will be more aroused than the other.

But the final statistic is the one that counts most: 40 percent of interactions will have both lovers being equally involved and aroused. Pretty good odds for having a lot of great sex!

CHAPTER 13

October

THE ALITALIA PLANE from Rome touched down at John F. Kennedy airport late on Thursday afternoon. Diana wanted to call Michael the minute she walked in the door of her apartment, but, applying her emotional brakes with all the discipline she could muster, she waited until the next morning, when she called him at his office and invited him for dinner.

"I'll be there as close to six as I can," he said in that

special, smiling voice she'd thought of so often in the past ten days. She could feel her heart beating as she hung up the phone.

Next she called the beauty salon.

"You're lucky, Miss Teague, Irene has a cancellation this morning. And I can fit you in with Lina right after that," said the pleasant voice of the receptionist.

Half an hour later Diana was esconced in a chair covered with flowered English chintz, her feet resting among the scalloped linen pillows that the salon used for the luxurious ritual of the pedicure. Irene, in a white coat, sat on a low stool, wielding the tiny steel cuticle clippers on Diana's toes with the single-mindedness of a surgeon. This procedure finished, she lathered Diana's legs in a rich pink creme and slowly massaged the muscles from heel to knee.

Half-hypnotized by the smooth kneading, Diana imagined Michael's blue eyes looking down at her; she saw the long, supple swimmer's body.

"What color polish would you like, Miss Teague?" Irene asked, bringing her back to reality.

"The brightest red you have. A clear, brilliant red!"

She closed her eyes to dream of Michael, feeling only the tiny, cool flicks of the brush as the crimson lacquer covered her toes.

"We can take you for your leg-waxing now, Miss Teague," said a voice from far away.

In the small, cream-colored waxing room Diana lay on a flat table made soft by a base of two lambswool blankets and two white sheets. The round pan of wax was placed, double-boiler style, in a pot of rolling water to keep it pliant. Lina slipped a diminutive pillow under her head and noiselessly began to swab Diana's legs with large cotton balls soaked in alcohol that smelled sharply of mint. The cooling effect of the alcohol and the expectation of the hot wax on her skin aroused her. She felt Michael's sexual touch all over her body—firm and soothing, insistent and unambiguous in its knowledge.

Lina expertly pulled the thin, wax-covered gauze strips, one after the other, off her legs, leaving the skin clear and soft as a summer fruit. It was an extravagant way to spend hard-earned money, but her whole body felt clean and lovely. Michael would like that. In a few hours she would be seeing him! Would he stay the night? Well, why wouldn't he?

By five thirty dinner was simmering on the stove, she had bathed, and was trying to decide what to wear.

Although she would describe her style as "conservative by nature," she was not immune to what she called male "triggers." Triggers, she had recently explained to her younger half-sister, were "what a man enjoys, gets excited by, gets thrown by." Take high heels, she had said. Those were a classic trigger.

And one to which even an outwardly conservative architect like Michael Boeting responded to.

"Oh, don't take those," he had said in Rome when she wanted to buy a sensible pair of medium-heel pumps, "Why don't you try these?" He was pointing

to high-heeled black and red sandals—more sexy
than elegant.

She bought them. She liked to please a man, wear
what turned him on—as long as she didn't feel com-
promised by it. She thought the sexy Roman shoes
were fun.

Now she wiggled her scarlet toes into them, leaning
over to adjust the red strap to her heel. What else to
wear? He'd be ringing the doorbell in a few minutes!
Her skin was still moist from the bath. She smoothed
the perfume he'd given her all over her body, put on
her best bra and bikini pants, decided on the white
silk dress to show off her Italian tan. Suddenly, grin-
ning at her recklessness, she abandoned the underwear the better to feel the sensuous, creamy silk of the
dress next to her bare, fragrant skin.

And suddenly he was there, his two hands holding
her face up to his to be kissed.

"Look, how wonderful your apartment is!" he ex-
claimed, still clasping her tightly to him while his keen
eyes measured the room.

"Since you're in such a handsome suit, you must
have come directly from the office. Are you tired?
Would you like some champagne?"

"No, I'm not tired, but I'd like to get out of this
tie—and I'd love some champagne!"

She led him into her small bedroom, pointed out
the bathroom and a place in the closet to hang his
jacket, and went to fetch some glasses.

"You didn't tell me you were such a good cook," he

said accusingly after they'd finished dinner and were still sitting at the table reminiscing about the inventiveness of Italian cuisine.

"Oh, there's lots more to learn about me," she answered in a teasing voice.

"Well, when can I start?" he retorted, smiling. And he took her hand, pulled her up from the table, and headed for the bedroom.

He had his clothes off before she even kicked off her sandals. He sprawled on the bed watching as the silk dress dropped to the floor.

"I like to look at you," he said contentedly. The light from the hall in back of him threw his body into sharp relief. She wasn't sure if he was conscious of his astonishing beauty or not.

He stretched out on her bed like a splendid lion, pulling her down on top of him and kissing her again and again. Then he turned on his side and pressed her compliant body into the crescent of his own warmth.

Slowly she began to be aware that something was missing. No swelling, no curving hardness insinuated itself between their bodies. Now he was kissing her expertly all over her neck, her shoulders, the small smooth space in the hollow of her back, the insides of her smooth legs. She touched his penis with her fingers and then took her hand away. The softness seemed so infinitely vulnerable.

Unlike many of her friends, she hadn't had many lovers, but all her experiences with sex—until Michael—had been straightforward and uncomplicated: she had never come across a penis that did not stiffen with desire. In Paris and Florence and Rome, Michael's penis was always rigid and lovely with its upward curve. Should she touch it again? Should she caress and hold it in her mouth? Should she try to lick it to life?

Michael was sucking at the tips of her breasts. Then he deftly shifted his body so that she was on top of him. She stroked the stone-smooth muscles of his chest and he sucked and licked at her nipples until they made the small little points that he said he loved. Now his fingers were moving knowledgeably inside her. Never stopping the searching, rhythmic pressure, he once again shifted his body so that he lay half on top of her, his fingers still deep within her.

Her clitoris vibrated under the smooth, knowing fingers. The strange, wonderful, feverish, floating feelings began to build. Her body opened, she thrust her pelvis toward him, wanting him to penetrate, to fill and steady her while she whirled and dissolved. Higher and higher and still higher his fingers took her. She felt like a wild kite soaring into deep space. At last she breathed in a deep rush of air; her body rocked back and forth in arcs of endless pleasure.

Slowly she let go of her breath, muscles still rigid. Michael was holding her against his powerful chest. The strength of his arms had a soothing effect as her body began to relax from the intensity of the orgasm. She knew he would be hard now. She reached down and, with fingers slithery from her own wetness, searched for his erection.

Something was still terribly wrong. What had she done? Could they make love only in exotic foreign cities? Could he not make love to her in New York because he was involved with someone else? What was the problem? What should she do?

Michael's face still looked unclouded, but she couldn't tell what storm might be building behind the guarded blue eyes. She kissed his chest and slid her kisses down his flat, hard stomach and into the soft, red-gold hairs that ringed his penis. She kissed it, licked it, enveloped it with her mouth. *It's not working.* Anxiety crouched at the base of her spine and then raced through her brain while she tried to concentrate on what she was doing.

"It's okay," she heard him say. He had his hands in her hair and was gently lifting her head from his body. "Let's just go to sleep." His arms were around her and his body curled around hers like a protective animal. In seconds his breathing was deep and even.

After an hour or so of deep sleep, she woke up, all her muscles tight and strained. They must talk about it. But he obviously hadn't wanted to say anything. He'd just gone straight to sleep. She disentangled herself from the warm legs that were flung over hers and replayed what had happened over and over again. But it would be different in the morning. They would make love in the morning, as they had done so many times in Europe. Calming herself with the idea that everything would be okay as soon as he woke up, she fell into a light, restless sleep.

He was out of bed.

She felt the warm spot where his body had been and opened her eyes. It was six-twenty.

"Michael, you're up so early. Let me get you a cup of coffee."

"I've got to get back to my apartment and get dressed for an eight-thirty meeting." He was tucking his shirttails in hastily. "I'll call you later." A light kiss on the lips and he was gone.

An early-morning meeting on Saturday?

Of course he wouldn't call her. She would never hear from him again. It was an out-of-this-world magical affair and it couldn't survive the everyday stresses of ordinary living.

She despised herself for doing it, but she waited all day for the phone to ring. At a few minutes before six she finally told herself, *call someone* and go to a good movie, then come home, cry it out, and *let it go!*

She had tried Alice and Jim earlier in the day, but they were out. Not expecting an answer, she dialed their number again. Alice was home. Jim had to work late in the office; he had a trial on Monday. Hearing her friend's voice, Diana burst into tears.

They caught an eight o'clock movie and later, over hamburgers and red wine, Diana told Alice of her marvelous short-lived affair.

"I hate to say this, but you know the men in this town—you probably won't hear from him again," Alice said. "He sounded too good to be true. But tell me the truth—haven't you ever come across a man who couldn't get it up?"

"I swear I never have."

"Well, let me tell you how I've dealt with the Problem . . . and it's a big problem," Alice said, and proceeded to pour out the reassurance that Diana needed so urgently the night before.

It was close to twelve when they left the coffee shop and Alice hailed a taxi to pick up Jim, who was still going over depositions at his office. Diana kissed her friend good night and felt connected to the world again. Michael Boeting was not the only person in her life.

She walked into her apartment and automatically switched the answering machine to Replay.

Don't kid yourself, she chided. That wasn't an *automatic* gesture; you're hoping against all reasonable hope that he's called.

Her heart stopped when a familiar voice said, "Di, it's Michael. I'm sorry I couldn't call you earlier. I had to go onto a site in Connecticut with my client. Can you have breakfast—at my place—tomorrow?"

She replayed the message four times.

CHAPTER 14

Erection Wreckers

"Shattered"

"Devastated"

"Wiped out"

"Crippled"

"Finished"

"I was thirty-three when it happened. I thought, I'm going to have to commit suicide."

The above words are from men who have experienced a one-time or sometime erection problem. Almost every man at some point in his life is unable to have or maintain an erection no matter how much he tries. The following fairly typical experience was told to me by a forty-year-old man who owns a car dealership in New Jersey.

"I had just begun an affair with a woman I thought I would eventually marry. I have always been sexually active and had never had a problem. Then one night wham! No hard-on. Now, I believe that I am a reasonably well-adjusted man, and I told myself that it was nothing to be concerned about—it happens to almost everyone. Then it happened again the next night. Kathy was terrific about it, said she loved me, and that everything would be okay. I felt I had failed her. I was certain I was finished, wiped out sexually, and I would never be able to function again. My mind told me that I was overreacting, but my feeling was one of complete dread about sex."

Erections are not under a man's control, and almost anything can trip up the physical/emotional balance that leads to sexual arousal. One of the most common erection-wreckers is alcohol. Another is too much food before sex. The *obligation* a man may feel to fulfill a partner's sexual needs can also block an erection. Stress, anger, medication, an uncaring and unresponsive woman—all these factors can stop the action.

An occasional or temporary erection problem is not impotence, but it can quickly skid into something serious if it's not handled with sensitivity and intelligence by both lovers. The reaction of a man who's had no history of erection problems ranges from acute anxiety the first time it happens to full-fledged fear if it continues. The more fear he feels, the more it will happen again as he tries to force himself to have an erection. Finally, he may turn off sex altogether in order to avoid the intense anxiety that overtakes him.

A woman often feels she is responsible for an erection problem. "I'm not attractive enough" or "I don't turn him on" are typical reactions. She too becomes anxious, which only makes the situation worse. *The fact is that a woman is rarely responsible for a man's erection failure.*

What can a woman do if the man she's with is having trouble?

First, remember it's not your fault. It's no one's *fault.* Don't ask *why.* There's no clear answer to the question, so don't try to dissect the situation; it can only provoke more anxiety. Be warm, loving, and let your attitude convey that the problem is not earthshaking. If the situation seems right for it, you might give him a back or neck massage and ask for one in return. It's a good way to maintain warm, affectionate body contact, get your minds off performance, and release tension at the same time.

If erection problems continue, then talking about it is the most helpful thing to do. Reassure your lover that everything is okay, that you know this must be difficult for him, that an erection is *not* a requirement for happiness. Therapists underscore that the point is to take his focus off performance and concentrate on enjoyment of each other.

A brief summary of the methods therapists are using to deal with erection problems might be helpful to both of you. Today the majority of practitioners follow some form of the original techniques developed by Masters and Johnson. As you will see, the aim is to sidestep "performance" and shine the spotlight on physical communication, relaxation, and pure pleasure. Here are the basic moves.

During the first few days you don't have intercourse, but you do focus on sensuous stroking of the body (excluding the breasts and the genitals) in a relaxed, unhurried atmosphere. Next comes oral and manual stimulation of the genitals. At this phase a man will usually have a spontaneous erection, but the couple is instructed not to have intercourse. However, if he doesn't have an erection, that's fine too. There's always tomorrow.

The next stage is basically a form of teasing. A man who's having an erection problem usually feels that he must put the erection to use immediately because he may never get one again. When an erection occurs during manual/oral stimulation, his lover is instructed to stop everything and deliberately allow the erection to subside. This kind of "teasing" is done several times in order to reassure a man that he can and will have regular erections.

In the final stages of therapy the woman sits astride

her lover. If he gets a full erection, she inserts his penis into her vagina. The idea behind this is to avoid any kind of performance anxiety. This step, like teasing, is repeated several times. Next, the woman begins to move so that the penis is further stimulated. If, however, the penis softens, fine. There's no pressure to have intercourse, and of course there's always a next time. If the penis stays erect, then the man can begin thrusting; orgasm may or may not happen, but it's not the point of the exercise—the object is feeling good. After a few "successful" experiences the erection difficulties are usually resolved.

Premature Ejaculation: Another Erection Wrecker

Many therapists report that premature ejaculation is the most common sexual complaint from men. Premature ejaculation has an insidious way of creating other problems. When a man comes too soon he worries about the problem constantly. The anxiety that it will happen quickly leads to erection problems and avoidance of sex. Thus, it's wise to deal with premature ejaculation as soon as possible. Fortunately it can be easily dealt with.

Two techniques, the "squeeze" (developed by James Semans) and "stop/start" (a version of the Semans technique used by Masters and Johnson) have been developed to help a man control his arousal level instead of allowing it to control him. The underlying idea is to teach a man to recognize the sensations he feels just prior to orgasm. Either of the following techniques can be done with a partner, but a therapist may advise that you first practice on yourself during masturbation.

Stop/start. You or your lover stimulate the penis manually until you feel the approach of the point of no return. Stop everything until your erection subsides and then start stimulation again. Repeat this until you're used to receiving as much stimulation as possible without ejaculating. With practice (over several days up to a couple of weeks), you'll find you need fewer and shorter pauses between stopping and starting until you can take extended stimulation without any pauses at all.

Squeeze. You or your lover stimulate the penis manually until you feel the approach of the point of no return. At this point, with the thumb on the sensitive strip of skin that joins the head to the shaft of the penis, and the first and second fingers on the top of the penis, squeeze for three or four or more seconds. The immediate urge to ejaculate will subside. Repeat this several times in one session. Again, with practice over several days, or even weeks, you'll begin to slow down and have control over ejaculation.

Note: In either technique if ejaculation has begun, don't try to stop it.

If you have sex infrequently or have been celibate for one reason or another, don't expect to have much success trying to control ejaculation until you've made love once or several times.

New Ways to Deal With Chronic Erection Problems

If a man has erection problems that are more than temporary or have become chronic, the first thing to do is see a doctor for a physical checkup. An erection problem can be physiologically or psychologically based. A doctor can test for erections during sleep. If you are having erections in the morning or while you sleep, the problem is probably not physical but psychological, and the best course of action is to talk to a qualified sex therapist.

The most recent research on erection problems concentrates on the physical causes. Today it's estimated that approximately 10 million American men are affected by impotence, which is clinically defined as the inability to have or maintain an erection satisfactory for intercourse. It's thought that about 50 percent of the cases are due to organic causes.

An erection is basically a hydraulic phenomenon. As a man becomes aroused, blood fills vessels in his penis, causing it to harden and rise. If, for example, a man is taking drugs that lower his blood pressure, he will probably have erection difficulties. This experience was told to me by a vivacious thirty-year-old publicist who works in San Francisco. "Paul and I have always been attracted to each other. But nothing's ever happened between us because we're both married. We found ourselves at a business convention in New York last year. We were staying at the same hotel and I went to have a drink in his suite. The room was beautiful, overlooking the whole city; it was truly romantic and the moment was right. At last we were going to bed together! But he couldn't get an erection. He explained to me that he'd been taking medication for a migraine headache and it lowered his blood pressure—and apparently everything else. We both laughed about it—what else could we do? He wasn't upset because he knew the problem would go away as soon as he stopped the medication the next day. But he was sad that we'd missed the perfect moment."

Many prescription drugs have side effects that lead to impotence and decreased sexual desire. A broad range of medications is now known to cause erection problems. Drugs for hypertension and diabetes, as well as antidepressants and antihistamines, are common erection-wreckers. See Chapter 20, Love-Drugs, for where to find out about specific medications that can cause erection difficulties.

Erection problems that were considered untreatable only a few years ago are yielding to new strategies and techniques. In the case of longstanding impotence, there is now the possibility of surgical penile implants which allow a man to have a firm erection. The devices are now sophisticated and, for the most part, undetectable.

Dr. E. Douglas Whitehead, a well-known urologist and founder of the Association for Male Dysfunction, says that today the "vast majority of patients with sexual dysfunction can be significantly helped in an approach that is rapid, convenient, and cost-effective." Should you need further information, call or write to the Association for Male Sexual Dysfunction, 520 East 72 Street, New York, NY 10021 (212) 794-1616.

CHAPTER **15**

Can We Talk?

"WHAT'S THE MOST IMPORTANT THING you've learned from your research about sex?" This is one of the most frequent questions that I'm asked. Before all else, *communication* is the vital, critical, crucial, essential ingredient in sex. "Communication" is so wildly overused and overexplained that I'm sick of the word. But the fact remains that one of the greatest problems in most relationships is the inability of the partners to ask for what they want and need.

"Talking about sex is bullshit," a man from Fort

Worth once told me. "If you have to talk about it, it's not good sex." The illogic behind this common but fossilized response is this: If you love someone, sex will be fine; if someone really and truly loves you, he or she will *know just what you want.* The truth is that loving someone does not make you a mind reader.

Of course there are nonverbal methods to communicate information about what you want or don't want. You can change positions, put a hand here, move a finger there. But ultimately, at some point in a sexual relationship, you're going to have to inform, discuss, suggest, advise, enlighten—in a word, *talk—* with each other about what you want and need.

If you don't communicate about what feels good or bad, what you crave or what you can't stand, what turns you on or off, you're likely to run into problems. You're going to feel

frustrated, anxious, angry, resentful

—emotional time-bombs, surefire love-killers. Sex and marriage counselors are quick to point out that often simply *talking* about a problem can improve things very quickly. "When we discuss things that have been bothering us, we immediately become closer. It feels as if I've been caressed and stroked. And it makes me want to make love," says a woman who learned the value of consistent, open communication at a marriage-encounter weekend.

The Risk/Reward Factor

Exactly why is it so difficult to discuss sex with your lover? Because you risk so much. You expose your deepest self in sex. In asking for a sexual favor, you risk ridicule, and, most frightening, you risk rejection. But if you want a sexual relationship to work, you must take those risks. Amazingly, you'll find that, when you let your lover know what you need and want, your requests will probably be met. Warmth, understanding, love, intimacy—the long-term rewards of clear communication are well worth the chances you take.

We've read enough in the last few years to know that men especially have difficulty in communicating feelings—that's a major cause of sexual gridlock. Even though much progress has been made in "opening men up," "strong-silent" conditioning can easily resurface in the sensitive area of sexuality. Thus, talking about sex or acknowledging that a problem might exist is for many men an admission of *failure* rather than the beginning of a resolution. The fact that things could be better indicates that he has failed as a lover, and, more deeply, failed as a man. When you see this in cold print, you realize how little sense it makes. When it comes to sex, reason is not always our strong suit.

Further reasons for silence: A man may be embarrassed talking about sex because he's out of his element ("women are the ones who do all the talking") or because he feels out of control. And a man, by (past) definition, should be in control.

Women, on the other hand, avoid talking about sex because they're afraid of *"hurting a man's feelings."*

This sadly typical experience was recounted to me by an attractive mother of three from Chicago:

We'd borrowed a friend's house on the lake in Michigan for the weekend and had been looking forward to sex without the kids being around. But when we got into bed, Jerry couldn't have an erection. It had happened a couple of times before but only when we'd had too much to drink. This time it was different. We were both primed for a great time, but we didn't talk about it. He's a good husband but a very private person. Sex is a very sensitive thing for a man, and I didn't want to hurt his feelings. We've never really talked about sex, even though there are some things that could be better for me. Anyway, I just let it slide, thinking that everything would be better when we got home. Things didn't get better, though, they got worse. Much worse. You may not believe this, but we didn't have sex for eight long months. I was tortured by the idea that he was having an affair, but I couldn't bring myself to say anything and even though I wanted us to see a therapist I felt he'd be angry if I suggested it. I know now that sounds crazy but that's how I felt.

Finally I was so desperate I called my gynecologist, who gave me the name of a marriage counselor. I felt sneaky and embarrassed about going, but all it took me was one short session to realize that we simply had to talk about what was going on. Well, finally we did air the problem. That little erection problem in Michigan was just the tip of the iceberg. We've gone through a lot of anger and tears, but the relationship is surviving. In fact, the only way it's going to survive is if we keep on talking. . . .

Another reason it's difficult for a woman to ask for what she wants sexually is that she's afraid a man will think she's too demanding, too aggressive (translate to: nonfeminine, nondesirable) or that she's very sexually experienced and therefore threatening or sluttish. Many woman whom I interviewed admitted that they would rather be sexually uncomfortable than risk the rejection they might face if they owned up to their sexual desires. "I masturbate just about every other day so I can have an orgasm. My husband just doesn't take the time I need. I've always praised his prowess as a lover. Am I going to do a turnaround now and tell him he's less than terrific? No way. I wouldn't want to risk my marriage," says one forthright woman who's settling for a lot less than she should.

How-to

This is obvious but needs to be said: Start communicating *as soon as possible.* If you're at the beginning of a relationship, both of you should make it clear right from the start what turns you on, what thrills you, what makes you anxious or embarrassed. If talking about sex has been always been off-limits, *it is never too late.*

Keep in mind that just as we all have different tastes and styles, we have different ways of communicating. You may want to dump everything out and talk, talk, talk. Your lover may be more laconic. It takes time and sensitivity to work out a communication pattern that suits you both.

First Step

Before you say one word to your lover, have a conversation with yourself. *Be scrupulously honest* or you won't be able to transmit your real feelings to someone else.

Ask yourself: What do I *really* want? (more/less oral/manual/anal sex, more direct stimulation, more hugging, kissing, romance, fantasy—whatever it is that you desire). Ask yourself: What am I not getting? Am I angry about it? Depressed, anxious, afraid? What about faking? Ask yourself: Does he know what I want? Do I know what *he* really wants? Once you've taken stock of where you stand, *have the confidence to accept your own desires.*

Mixed Messages

When you're initiating a discussion about sex, therapists advise that you talk about yourself first. Tell your lover your own needs, wishes, limitations, hang-ups. Then ask him/her to tell you what he thinks about what you've said. The point is to have an *exchange* of information between the two of you that leads to a clearer understanding of what you both want.

Talk between two lovers should be absolutely clear. Be specific: "I'd love you to do that" or "It feels a little too rough there" or "I'm worried that I don't know how to do oral sex the right way."

One of the easiest traps to fall into is the mixed message. Here are two of the most sexually common:

I'd love to make love but aren't you too tired?

Do you think it's too late to make love?

In both instances the message is unclear and confusing. Does the person want to make love or not? Simply saying, "I'd like to make love tonight" or "It's too late tonight, let's try for tomorrow" carries no confusing, hidden emotional freight.

Ask!

One autumn several years ago I spent a number of days freezing at 46 degrees without any heat in my so-called luxury apartment. Finally, when my son developed a bad cold, I stomped into the lobby and demanded to see the super. I don't like unpleasantness, and I'll do almost anything to avoid a confrontation, but by the time the super came up from his desk in the basement I was in a rage.

"Don't you know there's a law that says you have to put the heat on when it's below fifty degrees? Why don't you get the boiler fixed," I almost shouted.

"There's nothing wrong with the boiler."

"What about *the law*? Don't you know about the law?"

He admitted to knowledge of the law.

"Then why in hell isn't the heat on?"

"Nobody *asked* me to put it on," he said.

Two hundred people occupied the building. Many families, dozens of children. Not one person had asked. Everyone just assumed the boiler was broken and hadn't approached the super.

The moral of this tale is: *Ask questions and don't assume anything.* When it comes to sex, this axiom holds especially true. "I thought my husband hated to give me oral sex," one woman told me. "He didn't like the way I smelled or something. And I really love it. I finally asked him what it was that turned him off about doing it. He looked amazed and told me he thought that *I* didn't like it."

Ask what your lover likes, ask what could make it better for him/her. If you're worried that you're not pleasing your lover sexually, or you're not getting what you'd like, *ask.* The answers may surprise you.

The other side of communication is listening. According to communications experts, most of us listen at about 25 percent efficiency. How many times have you heard, "He (or she) doesn't listen to me!" A good listener/lover

> does not assume that he knows what a person means
> does not interrupt
> avoids making judgments
> is not defensive
> does not jump to conclusions.

In short, the idea is to transmit the feeling that you have something to *learn* from what the other person is saying. "Your attitude is so important when you talk about sex. Keep your mind open. So many people tune out because they're afraid of hearing something that will upset them. Most times this is not the case. Approach talking with your lover as a learning experience, points out a marriage counselor. "You're going to benefit from it, not be hurt."

Another useful idea from the same therapist: "The best way to avoid becoming angry and defensive is to *concentrate* on what the other person is saying. When you've really heard what he or she has to say, then you can give yourself time to think and respond. That's the way you can begin to make meaningful changes."

If You Run Into THE WALL

The Wall is the negative response or no response at all. "Problem, what problem?" is a form of The Wall. "Nothing's bothering me" or "I'm not angry" are other versions.

Before you start to sizzle, consider this (I'm using the pronoun "he" here, but "she" would be just as appropriate): Your lover may not be in touch with his feelings. He may truly not be aware of the problem that's causing you so much anguish. Give him time to come to terms with what you've told him and say that you'd like to talk it over again when he's had a chance to think it through.

If he says "nothing's wrong" and you feel there is something definitely amiss, don't persist—it just blocks further communication—but do try again later. If he *still* doesn't respond, you might say, "Okay, you may think nothing's wrong and you're not upset, but here's what's bothering me. Let's try and deal with it."

If he claims he's not angry, and you're pretty sure that he is, don't press the point. Instead, try saying, "I believe what you tell me. But if you ever are angry with me—and we all get angry—please let's talk about it before it makes a big rift between us."

I was discussing the difficulties of communication with an articulate, attractive, thirty-three-year-old Manhattan writer. "Did you ever," he said with a teasing smile, "suggest to your readers that they ask each other the questions you have just asked me? What's good sex? What's great sex? Everyone has different ideas on the subject, as you well know. It would be a terrific way to get a provocative conversation going and to compare what each partner thinks sex is all about. I'll bet there are people who have been married for years who don't know what their spouses think about sex."

What to Say When . . .

The following are typical problems that most of us find difficult to handle, and some simple ideas and answers that you may find helpful and effective in dealing with them.

HOW TO SAY NO WITHOUT HURT FEELINGS

The tides of desire ebb and flow because of psychological reasons as well as biological ones. If you've established clear, understanding communication, you should be able to tell each other lovingly that you're just not in the mood for sex. It's human, normal, and perfectly okay for two people to have differing sexual energy.

Nonetheless, saying no to sex can be a tricky issue for both of you because it's subject to all kinds of misinterpretations and hurt feelings if it's not handled sensitively and intelligently.

Most people, as a matter of fact, don't say no. They use a variety of techniques to avoid the issue. Picking a fight is the most common. If you're irritated at your mate, there's little chance that he or she will want to make love. A second method is to pretend you're already asleep or that you don't recognize your lover's advances because you're too busy doing something important.

Such evasive maneuvers don't work. They're a direct route to anger and resentment. The first rule of thumb to saying no is to tell the truth. You might try putting it this way: "I'm really tired, I've had an extra-specially tough day." Or, simply, "I'm just not in the

mood right now . . ." The sensitivity lies in adding
". . . but let's make a date to make love tomorrow
night" (or tomorrow morning, or this weekend, etc.).
It's hard to feel rejected if your partner is already
setting the rain date.

Perhaps the most direct and amusing way of saying
no that I heard was from a woman whose husband
had been under exceptional career stress. "I just can't
do it tonight," he said to her when she started making
love to him. *"My penis is racked with tension!"*

WHAT TO DO IF YOUR LOVER ASKS YOU TO DO SOMETHING THAT MAKES YOU UNCOMFORTABLE

Again, tell the truth. Say what bothers you about it:
"I'm embarrassed" or "It makes me feel dirty" or "I've
never done that before and I'm anxious about it."
Keep an open mind and say that you're not ready for
that—*yet.* Then try this version of the visualization
exercise outlined on page 56.

Visualize, in detail, the act that upsets you. Say, for
example, it's oral sex. At the moment that you start to
feel tense (your mouth touching penis or vagina),
drop the mental picture and concentrate on deep,
even, relaxing breathing. As soon as you're calm, start
to visualize the troublesome area again. Alternate
your calming technique with visualizing until you can
mentally picture the act without tensing.

If you run into trouble when you actually try it, tell your partner you're anxious and you've gone as far as you can go this time. Next time you're going to take it one step further. Few lovers will be unsympathetic to such an honest and sensitive admission of anxiety.

WHEN YOU'RE ABSOLUTELY AGAINST DOING WHAT YOUR LOVER WANTS

When you're absolutely against what she/he is asking for, tell your partner it's just not for you, but offer an explanation: "I feel too uptight about doing that." Or, "I was brought up in a strict religious way, and it makes me anxious to think of doing that." State exactly what the *truth* is for you. When you're straightforward about your hang-ups and anxieties, you'll probably be amazed at how understanding your partner will be.

IF YOUR LOVER IS GOING TOO FAST

When *he* goes too fast and speeds up lovemaking it may be because he's afraid of losing his erection, and, if he's like most men, he would never want to admit it. The best way to handle this is to tell him frankly that you need more time to be aroused, and if he'd like to come, great, but you'd love some more stimulation afterward. You might also tell him you've read about a technique that slows things down (see page 135) and how about some delicious experimenting?

When *she* goes too fast and wants him to come right away, the likeliest reason is that she's angry or resentful and is expressing it by denying her lover pleasure. Another reason might be that she's anxious about sex and is probably having trouble with (or faking) orgasm. Ask—gently—what the hurry is. Tell her how much you'd like extended lovemaking— what are her ideas on the subject? Ask her how you could make it more pleasurable for her. If you sense she's angry or resentful in some way, block out time (*not* in bed) to have a discussion about what's causing the hostility.

IF YOU'VE BEEN FAKING

Of the women I've interviewed, approximately 60 percent admitted to faking orgasm some of the time. But there is a sad and sizable group that fakes most if not all of the time. "In the great majority of cases where this happens," points out a marriage counselor, "it would be a dangerous mistake to just blurt out the truth to your husband. I would first advise some deep soul-searching. *Why* are you faking? Are you angry or depressed? Why do you want to create distance from your partner? These are difficult questions, and in most cases the answers should be analyzed with the help of a competent therapist."

Men fake too. "I'm sometimes just too tired to go

on," admits a man who is constantly under business pressure, "so I've faked a few times. My wife doesn't know—she's never said anything about it—so what's the difference?" The difference can develop into a nasty situation—faking on any level is antithetical to intimacy. Why not say, "I'd love to make love tonight but I'm beat"? Women don't expect men to be non-stop sex machines, and a man who honestly tells his lover he's tired or just not up to it at the moment is sowing the seeds for healthy intimacy.

IF YOU'D LIKE HER TO MAKE THE FIRST MOVE MORE OFTEN

Ask her how she feels about taking the initiative in lovemaking. She may be afraid you'll think she's being too aggressive. Tell her you'd enjoy a seductive, aggressive woman and you'd love her to make the first move.

IF SHE'S SHY/RETICENT AND YOU WANT TO LIVEN THINGS UP—FAST

A tall, woman-loving sculptor in New York says, "I love a woman to suggest things, but unfortunately not many women do. So I sometimes say, 'What are you going to do to me tonight?' If the answer is 'Everything,' I say, 'Tell me specifically—tell me in detail.' It always turns out to be a turn-on for both of us."

IF YOU'D LIKE TO TAKE THE LEAD WITH HIM

He's been the active one in the relationship and you'd like to take the lead—at least some of the time. Ask him how he feels about being seduced. Ask him how he'd react if you made love to him. You might say something like, "How would you like me to make love to *you* tonight?" Based on all my research, I can tell you very few men would turn down the offer.

IF YOU'RE A SHY WOMAN AND YOU'D LIKE TO BE MORE ACTIVE IN LOVEMAKING

Tell him in advance you're thinking along new lines. You might say, "I'd like to try something special tonight. Expect to have a really romantic evening."

If you've never been the initiator and you're worried that he'll think you're too agressive or wonder where you got the idea, tell him what one wise woman I interviewed told her husband: "I read in a book that men like women who make the first moves some of the time." If he's like the majority of men, he'll be delighted.

IF YOU WANT MORE—OR BETTER—ORAL SEX

Ask how he/she feels about oral sex. Explain that you'd like more and say *why.* "It's one of the most intimate things you can do for me." Or, "It is so sensational. There's no other feeling like it." Or, "It makes me feel truly loved." Or, "It gives me a knockout orgasm." Then say you'd like to show her/him how it feels best for you.

IF YOU ARE TURNED OFF BY INSTRUCTIONS

"I feel like I'm being directed by a traffic cop. Go a little to the right—a little to the left—slower—faster. I want to give my girlfriend what she wants, but it's getting to be too much," grumbled a man who was being told in no uncertain terms what turned his girlfriend on. It's a common reaction, particularly from males—they don't like being told what to do. But specific instructions are truly valuable; they let you know exactly what feels best to your lover. When you're giving directions you can also give a lot of positive feedback: "There, *that* feels great! Yes, that's the spot . . . that's the exact rhythm!" Even if you're not thrilled by being given directions, try it for a night or two; the destination should make it worth your while.

IF YOU WANT TO KNOW/TELL ABOUT SEXUALLY TRANSMITTED DISEASES

Many men and women ask straightforwardly, "Do you have any diseases that I should know about?" But a more gentle way might be the one suggested to me by a trim, worldly television executive. "I was burned once, but I still find it difficult to be direct about venereal disease or herpes," she says. "I prefer saying to a man, 'I really like you and I believe you would tell me if there's anything wrong.' Or, 'If you have any health problems, you *would* tell me, wouldn't you?'"

"The best advice I was given on the subject actually came from my gynecologist," another woman said. "This doctor said, in essence: Take his penis in your hand and stroke it, examine every part of it. Give him compliments, tell him you love the way he looks, but be looking under, over, and all around while you're fondling. If you see something unusual, ask, 'What's this? Did you know this was here?' I once asked a man about a large sore that he had on his penis, and he said, 'Oh, it's always been there.' I just didn't believe him and said I didn't think I could sleep with him. He stomped out angrily, but my health is more important."

Another sensitive solution: If you suspect problems, you can ease some of the discomfort he might be feeling by putting the burden on yourself and saying, "My diaphragm (or IUD or the Pill) is giving me problems and I've got to have it checked. Would you mind using a condom tonight?"

CHAPTER 16

The Great Frequency Debate

How Often Is Everyone Else Doing It— and What If You're Not Doing It at All?

I WISH I'd kept count of times I've been asked this question: "My husband (or my wife) doesn't want to make love as much as I do. What should I do?"

Questions involving frequency and desire are one of the most flammable areas in a relationship. The highly respected Blumstein and Schwartz study has shown that the more frequently a couple makes love, the more satisfied they are sexually. But frequency differs from couple to couple. One couple may think twice a week is frequent while another defines the word as meaning sex every day. The Blumstein/ Schwartz study also shows that most married couples have sexual relations at least once a week, and even after a decade of marriage about two out of every three couples still have sex that often.

Sex drive is a fascinating part of our personality that is not fully understood. As of this writing, these are the facts we have.

Each of us has a different level of interest in sex, and, to make things more complicated, that drive differs daily, weekly, monthly, and yearly. Hormones affect sex drive. The majority of women are aroused most easily, lubricate most quickly, just prior to menstruation, not during ovulation as we previously thought. For men, the level of testosterone (which helps to dictate sexual response), appears to be at its peak in the early morning. (Note for extra-long-distance runners: Recent findings confirm that running over fifty miles per week lowers sexual response in males.—the *New York Times*, June 22, 1984)

A man's sexual flame burns hottest and brightest in his late teens and early twenties, so it's not surprising that the men who complain that their wives are not as interested in sex as they would like them to be tend to be in their twenties. If you marry in your early twenties, it's not unlikely to find that he may want sex once a day or even more, while she's perfectly satisfied with two or three times a week.

A woman is at the height of sexual interest from her

mid to late thirties through her early forties, so by that time the roles are likely to be reversed if she's married to a man close to her own age. She may be interested in sex three or four or even more times a week, and he's the one who's likely to plead the proverbial headache at bedtime.

According to the most recent research, heredity plays an important part in sexual appetite. It may be that you are genetically more interested in sex than your partner. "I always felt I was born randy. I was initiated into sex at twelve and I haven't slowed down," says an intensely sexual artist, now in his early forties.

Biology is a definite factor, but subtle psychological factors can be even more central to the ebb and flow of sex drive/desire. The *importance* you give to sex is critical to frequency. If you feel that sex is important to your relationship (and you'd be foolish if you thought it wasn't!), you're going to have more of it.

Another primary factor in sex drive is your state of mind and the amount of stress you're under. If you're worrying about how your body looks, whether the mortgage payments will be made, why your child isn't doing well at school, you're certainly not going to be as interested in sex as you would be with an uncluttered mind focused solely on pleasure. Exactly how do you unclutter your mind? Exercise is one obvious answer. Concentration is another. Concentrate on detaching your mind as much as possible from outside pressures, say the experts. Use relaxation techniques such as deep breathing or meditation, or just take a long hot soak. Controlling stress is infinitely easier said than done, but it's absolutely necessary if your sex life is to survive!

Is it possible to reconcile being on different sexual wavelengths? Yes, say therapists and marriage counselors. The best solution is negotiation and compromise. If he likes a quickie in the morning and she prefers long, leisurely lovemaking at night or on the weekends, one simple, easy resolution is to try taking turns. Another common stalemate is when he'd like to make love almost every day and she's interested only in once or twice a week. A "negotiated settlement" in this instance might involve "quality lovemaking" once or twice a week and pure physical quickie-sex to relieve tension and/or horniness the other times.

Frequency, to most people, equals the number of times the penis goes into the vagina. But sex really includes touching, giving massages, taking showers together, as well as oral sex, manual sex, and masturbation. The frequency issue is far easier to work out if you accept all these options and consider them "sex" just as you do intercourse.

"I'm Just Not Interested in Sex Anymore . . ."

It can happen to anyone at any time—you just aren't so turned on anymore. This is how one man describes the feeling: "My wife is in good shape, she goes to exercise classes, she has a great new job, she's an interesting person—but I'm just not interested. It's a kind of apathy and it's gone on for *three* months. I don't feel bored or depressed, but I don't feel like having sex and it frightens me." This forty-year-old man is suffering from what therapists call lack of desire.

Both men and women can be hit by this sexual malaise. Some therapists estimate that up to 50 percent of their patients suffer from it. Most are married, but no one is immune. What causes someone to lose interest in sex? The reasons are complex and far-reaching, but there are several basic factors that can be easily pinpointed. The first and most common reason for lack of interest in sex is hidden anger. You turn off simply because at some level, either very deep or near to the surface, you resent and feel angry at your mate. "It's impossible to make love to someone with whom you're angry. It's a contradiction in terms. You can force yourself, but it's obviously going to backfire at some point," states a marriage counselor.

Depression, which is closely linked to anger, also reduces desire, as does guilt—both of which can be deep-rooted and may be difficult to recognize.

Lack of sexual understanding is another culprit. When I've closely questioned a woman who has turned off to sex, it often turns out she (and usually her partner) have some misconceptions of what sex is all about. She is not being made love to in a way that she needs—meaning that her partner may not know how much romance, affection, touching, and time are central to a woman's sexual arousal. Even if a woman does know what she needs sensually/sexually/emotionally, she may be timid or hesitant about telling her partner. "I was afraid he'd be turned off if I told what I really wanted. I thought he'd feel he was a bad lover. Sex became such a letdown that I finally just tuned out," said one woman with tears in her eyes who told me she hadn't had sex with her husband in *three years.*

Still another sad and common situation stems from sexual misinformation. It usually takes this form: A man who is about fifty seems to lose interest in sex. His wife, who is a few years younger than he, says that they've had a pretty fine sex life, and now he doesn't want to do it at all.

In fact, he hasn't lost interest—it's been submerged under that old male bugaboo, performance fear. A man in his fifties may notice he's not getting an erection as fast as he once did. He begins to fear impotence, or he tells himself he's slowing down and better to leave the sex stuff to the kids. Or, more disastrously, he tells himself that a new, younger woman is what he needs to get his interest up. His wife notices the cool-off, but it's never really discussed. Neither has recognized the fact that a man of fifty may just need more direct genital stimulation. Usually he's afraid to ask for it, while his wife, who also lacks sexual sophistication and has been used to his having regular erections, decides that he doesn't desire her anymore. The fact is simply that he needs more time and more direct oral/manual stimulation to be aroused.

What can be done about lack of sexual interest? Once again, communication—and an awareness of physical needs and changes—could forestall serious problems if done *early enough*. Exchanging your feelings is an invaluable way to deal with the anger and depression that is usually at the root of lack of desire. Sometimes simply by talking about your hostility—not dumping it out but explaining clearly and nonaggressively what you're experiencing—can dissolve a sexual block or turn around a mild depression. You'll find that most negative feelings stem from feeling hurt, unloved, unrespected. Anger and resentment also arise from nonsexual issues like career problems or a perception that housework and child-care responsibilities have been delegated unequally or are being badly handled.

One simple and useful exercise (B. W. McCarthy, in *Journal of Sex and Marital Research,* Summer 1984) you can try is this:

Tell your partner what you find appealing and attractive about her/him. Your mate's role here is to *listen and acknowledge* what you're expressing. He or she cannot deny or dismiss what you've said by statements such as "That's not so" or "I'm not really attractive."

After you've told your partner the areas that you find appealing about her/him, you make two or three specific requests for changes that will make her/him more attractive to you. These requests can be sexual or nonsexual. For example, "Please don't smoke (or drink, or eat) so much." Or, "I'd like to make this change about the way we have sex."

Now reverse the roles with your partner and let her/him tell you what's appealing/attractive and then request one to three changes that will improve the picture even more.

You may be able to cope with lack of sexual interest if you deal with it as soon as possible. Unfortunately, most couples usually allow the problem to become entrenched for *years*. If this is the case, it's wise for one or both of you to seek qualified professional help to get to the root of the problem.

CHAPTER 17

Four Months Later

THEY HAD BEEN LIVING TOGETHER for four months when Michael told her he had had a homosexual experience.

"It was in Los Angeles, a few years ago," he said. "I was working as an assistant to an architect while I was in my first year of graduate school. Most of his projects were interiors, decorating really. So I was often at the Design Center, where a lot of gays staffed the showrooms.

"I was always vaguely curious about what it would be like to have sex with someone who is physically the same as I am, but never curious enough or interested enough to pursue the idea. Then I went to a party at the Design Center. I had a date who was supposed to go with me, but she canceled at the last minute.

"It was a pretty wild and woolly party and I had a lot of grass. There were very few women around, and after a while I began to dance by myself. I was really worked up, and all I wanted was hot straight sex. As it worked out I got the sex, but it wasn't straight. The strange thing was I didn't feel strange about it. The next morning I simply chalked it up to an interesting—and unusual—sexual experience, nothing more or less. I've never done it with a man since—my curiosity was satisfied and I never had the desire to."

Diana was lying in bed the morning after their conversation about past loves while Michael was out running. *The New York Times* was strewn over the covers, but she felt too distracted to read. In addition to learning about Michael's experience with a man, Diana had finally found out who it was he'd telephoned from their hotel room in Paris. Her instincts had been right on target: it *was* a woman, the woman he'd been living with for almost two years. They had just split up, but he had called to wish her happy birthday. Again, Diana could hear that low, intimate voice he'd used with her.

It was totally irrational, but just thinking of that phone call made her crazy with jealousy.

She kept going over last night's dialogue, trying to sort out her feelings. Was she threatened by the thought of *Michael with another man?* Did it somehow tarnish him?

No on both counts, she could honestly admit to herself. She believed him when he said he had no further desire for a man, and she didn't feel that consuming jealousy that burned at her when she thought of Margo. The truth was that she too had occasionally wondered how it would feel to make love to another woman. Like Michael, she was curious about what another body exactly like hers would feel like—but if faced with the reality of being in bed with such a body, she would have lost her courage.

Making love with two *men,* if one of those men were Michael—now *there* was a situation that, surprised though she was by her own feelings, intrigued her: the possibilities seemed endlessly fascinating.

She took a sip of lukewarm coffee and set the breakfast tray on the floor next to the bed. Closing her eyes, she thought of a young Michael in Los Angeles. She imagined, not a gay party in the Design Center, but a pale, cool bedroom. She sees two beautiful men, one kneeling before the other, both bare-chested, their taut muscles sheened with perspiration.

Standing, Michael opens his white jeans, revealing swollen, throbbing flesh. The kneeling one opens his mouth slowly, deliberately, slowly. The brush of his dark mustache mingles with stiff, curling, reddish-blond hairs. The full, sensuous lips open and move slowly to Michael's penis. The mouth moves down the rigid shaft, lapping, licking, sucking, moving faster and faster as two hands clasp the massing, tightening sphere below.

Quickly Michael takes his hard, glistening penis from the mouth, his supple sinewy hands urgently grip the dark-haired man's hard, round buttocks, the finger seeks to pierce the small, tight bud that lies hidden behind; the expert finger, wet with saliva, finds its point, forcing it to open. Then suddenly Michael is thrusting into that glistening, anointed hole. Now the dark-haired man's long, lean, muscular legs are thrown over Michael's golden shoulders. Michael pushes harder and deeper. The dark-haired man is moving his own oiled, hard cock faster and faster with his own hands. It is about to burst. He begins to move in quick, jerking spasms. He is groaning while Michael jams himself in harder and deeper, like a magnificent animal resplendent in his conquest. The room is shimmering with white-hot sex; sweat makes rivulets along the hard, potent bodies.

A woman opens the door, inhales the fevered smell of sex. She begins to take off her clothes, never moving her cool gray eyes from the two men, now lying at rest on the bed. She has a magnificent polished body, the globes of her buttocks round and smooth like summer fruit, her breasts high and proud. She stands over Michael, and his sapphire eyes are mesmerized by her slow, languid movements.

She places one hand on his shoulder and then

easily, gracefully, mounts him, her long, perfectly formed legs stretched over his. She moves her lustrous body in small, undulating motions so that her skin, her breasts with the delicate tracing of blue veins, are washed with his sweat. She slides her body down his so that her mouth envelops his penis. Lazily, she laps her tongue around it, savoring the acrid, mingled semen from both men. He feels the quickening as she holds the skin taut at the base, her mouth skillfully coaxing and cajoling and sucking it to life. Expertly her hands massage the tender, promising skin that is close to the tightened, unpenetrated bud. Slowly she reaches in, feels him contract and then relax, her finger now seeking the rounded gland of ultimate pleasure.

As her mouth and hands whirl him into an infinite wave of feeling, the dark-haired man has moved so that he is standing near her gleaming back at the foot of the bed. His penis is thick with wanting her. Over her heaving shoulders the dark-haired man can see Michael's eyes closed in the sexual rapture that she is slowly, expertly, relentlessly giving to him. The dark-haired man places a hand on her breast, stroking the nipple. His other hand seeks the opening between her legs. He feels the slithery wetness and parts the full buttocks, thrusting his long, thick penis deep inside her. She makes no sign except for the interior constricting and loosening of her vagina. But this tightening of her clasp on him drives him into a frenzy.

Michael's breathing hastens as he sees her penetrated, as he feels the thrusts into her body above him. Her breath is coming in small gasps now as she takes his penis out of her mouth, leaves it pulsating, distended, and starts to bite—small, sharp bites down his neck, on to his heaving chest, quickly down the raised veins and muscles of his legs and back to his throbbing, stinging shaft. Again she opens her mouth to it, gripping, vibrating, biting, sucking, the suction wrenching deep, low, groans of ecstasy from him.

The dark-haired man falls on the woman's sinuous back again, and now his thrusts go deeper and deeper as he feels her body convulse from the force of Michael's violent climax.

As her body rhythmically contracts beneath the dark-haired man's curving, pushing penis, her swollen breasts reach toward Michael's mouth. He suckles her—hard—and reaches down to find her nerve center quivering and begging for his hand. And now his penis is stiffening again, and he thrusts it into her mouth as the other man pierces to the bottom of her pulsating, contracting womb. Her clitoris is throbbing, heat is flooding through her body, the dizzying circles of her pleasure widen and widen, deep in her body at the edges of her being, in the chasm of her soul, she is screaming as she comes again and again and again as she has never come before . . .

Amazed at the vividness of her fantasy, Diana forces herself to relax and slowly drifts off to sleep, the images still swirling beneath her closed lids.

To be continued . . .

CHAPTER 18

The New Frontier

ONE DAY several years ago, before I started researching sexuality, I had to hurry uptown for an early morning appointment. The subway was rush-hour-jammed, and after several minutes of jolting and lurching I was lucky enough to squeeze into a just-vacated seat. I opened my *New York Times* but found myself in the clutches of an unwonted distraction. I couldn't help staring directly into blue-jeaned, beige-twilled, and gray-flanneled crotches that were precisely at eye level, swaying to and fro in the rocking rhythms of the uptown E train. I wondered what it would be like if I just reached out my hand and unzipped one. What lay behind the tantalizing bulge of the blue serge? How deliciously insolent the fullness of the button-front Levi's appeared. What would happen if I simply unbuckled, unzipped, reached inside . . . *Stop, stop, stop!* I jammed on the mental brakes, the discipline and teachings of many years rescued me from any further subterranean wanderings and I forced myself to go back and concentrate on the Op-Ed page.

Fantasies, especially sex fantasies, had always been absolutely off-limits for me. I was brought up with the notion that a person who daydreamed or fantasized a lot was frustrated, or making up for shortcomings, or just plain lollygagging. In short, daydreams and fantasies were one whopping waste of valuable time. And *sexual* fantasies—why, they were even more degenerate, and if not stopped immediately they could be *dangerous*, for who knew where they might lead!

There's been a dramatic and fascinating turnaround in the years since I took that subway ride. We've known about the importance of fantasies since Freud, but the most recent findings in the field indicate that fantasies are important keys to healthy sexual functioning and can reveal a great deal about a couple's relationship. The most interesting news, however, lies in the ways you can *use* fantasy. It can open up a whole new world of communication, it can spark a whole new kind of turn-on, and it's a new and wonderfully effective tool to tune up a slowed-down sex life.

How, specifically, can fantasies help change your love life? Before that intriguing question can be answered you'll need a brief rundown on what researchers have found out about our most intimate imaginings.

Most of us have seven or eight sexual fantasies per day. But it's not abnormal to have none or as many as forty. Some researchers feel that a lower rate of fantasizing appears to occur after age thirty-five.

What are the most frequent fantasies? (From the *New York Times*, February 28, 1984)

For men:
1. Replacement of established partner
2. Forced sexual encounters with woman
3. Observing sexual activity
4. Sexual encounters with men
5. Group sex

For women:
1. Replacement of established partner
2. Forced sexual encounters with man
3. Observing sexual activity
4. Idyllic encounters with unknown men
5. Sexual encounters with women

Interestingly, there's no difference between men and women when it comes to the number of fantasies they have. Indeed, the three most common fantasies are shared by both sexes. Usually men and women imagine someone they know as a new lover, but about 30 percent fantasize about an unknown partner.

The category of forced sexual encounters can be most misleading. Therapists are quick to point out that an imagined rape scene usually has an idealized, perhaps even romantic, quality to it. "It's a willing rape that really isn't rape at all," is how one marriage counselor characterized a forced sexual encounter. When researchers actually showed tapes of a realistic rape situation that included the violence that is inherent in rape, there was no arousal at all. Therapists explain that a romanticized, forced sexual encounter may relieve guilt about sex—it's a way of giving oneself permission to enjoy sex since you have none of the responsibility.

Thus it's no surprise that women fantasize more passive roles, while men's fantasies include both active and passive roles. Men imagine more kinds of sexual acts than women do, but women's fantasies are more specific, more elaborate, more detailed, and include a great deal of caressing.

According to the latest thinking, fantasies—even unconscious ones—can make you more willing to be sexual. In short, they inspire desire. If you fantasize frequently and in an uninhibited way—meaning you don't stop, monitor, or restrict yourself—you're healthy and probably have relatively few hang-ups about sex. The more clinical way to say it is "sexual fantasizing is positively correlated to a satisfying sex life." (D. Zimmer, E. Borchardt, and C. Fischle, in *Journal of Sex and Marital Therapy*, Spring 1983)

Another fascinating finding that should set many minds at ease is that both straight men and women fantasize about homosexual sex and that both gay men and women fantasize about straight sex. (Mark Schwartz and William Masters, *American Journal of Psychiatry*, January 1984) If you weave fantasies about gay sex, it does not mean you're a latent homosexual; you're just dreaming in a perfectly normal way.

What are fantasies used for?

How can they change your sex life?

These are the key questions that are currently being posed by researchers. And even the early answers are wonderfully useful.

Primarily, fantasies facilitate sexual arousal: *They turn you on.* And you can use these turn-ons to rev up, spruce up, and spice up a sagging sex life. To put it in more "serious" terms: Some therapists today believe that sexual fantasies can be used to alter patterns of sexual arousal and sexual behavior. What this means specifically is that you can take a less-than-perfect situation and make it much, much better if you use some fantasy.

For example, if you'd like to make love with your husband/wife and you're just not aroused, there's nothing wrong in consciously imagining Jamie Lee Curtis in a drop-dead bikini or Sam Shepard kissing you passionately to get yourself going. Dr. Mark

Schwartz, a marital/sex therapist in New Orleans and former director of research at the Masters and Johnson Institute, puts it this way (interview, the *New York Times*, February 28, 1984): "If a man loses his arousal while making love with his wife and uses a fantasy to get it back, then lets go of the fantasy to focus on the lovemaking again, it's irrelevant what the fantasy is about. It's a helpful bridge back to making love and increases the couple's intimacy."

Many therapists are now advising women who have trouble with orgasms to read erotic books and look at erotic pictures or films to build up their fantasy repertoire. Recent research also shows that men as well as women who are distressed sexually have fewer fantasies and interrupt them as well as negating the enriching qualities they may possess. These people are depriving themselves of a good deal of pleasure. Increasing fantasizing skills is a highly useful tool in beating the widespread malaise of lack of sexual desire.

The downside to all the good news about fantasy is this: If you *must* fantasize every time you make love, or if you find that you can't let go of a fantasy during lovemaking, you're not using fantasy in a healthy way. Rather than fantasizing to arouse yourself, or to overcome the temporary liabilities of a given situation, you're probably using fantasy to maintain or increase the distance between you and your partner, and it's an indication that the relationship is in trouble.

From Polaroids to Passion Tapes

What more can you do with fantasies?

Plenty.

If you've never actually done anything with your fantasies and you and your lover just want to dip your toes into the swirling, surprising, sensuous deep sea of the imagination, there's one important prerequisite: *trust.* Mutual respect and the willingness to explore new areas of your own and your partner's sexuality are also essential.

Telling each other your sexual fantasies is one of the most intimate experiences you can have, and can be a major turn-on. It's also a nonthreatening way to give your partner valuable information about ways of making love that you might enjoy. Some therapists suggest writing your fantasies down and exchanging them with your lover: it's a way of giving each other intimate knowledge that you might be uncomfortable talking about.

An attractive male art director from Los Angeles uses fantasies as a highly stimulating and provocative sexual aid. "I think creativity is critical to great sex. I often ask my lover to tell me a story. She has several scenarios. Maybe she's at a cocktail party and she's met a movie star she's been secretly in love with since she was a teenager." I say to her, "Tell me exactly what happened after you met him . . ." and she'll go on to describe how he seduced her, where he took her, what he did to her. The man in the story symbolizes what I'd like to be at that moment: aggressive, handsome, virile. I get steamed up with all of this and so does she. Sex is fantastic after one of those tales . . . I also learn a lot about her secret desires from the stories. And so does she."

Acting out your own scenarios—taking fantasies out of your head and making them happen—is another way to open up the lines of communication, and one that more and more couples are using. Your acting out of a fantasy can range from something as simple as wearing a garter belt or a new nightgown to elaborate scenes that take props and pre-planning.

An artist whom I interviewed told me that he had a fantasy of long standing that involved three-way sex: he wanted to make love to two women and have two women make love to him. After he was married he told this to his wife, who was fascinated with the idea. He describes his experience with making a fantasy into a reality:

One Sunday afternoon I was laid up in bed with a sprained ankle watching baseball on TV. Liza, my wife, came home with a girlfriend of hers that I had always thought was a knockout. They sat on the bed with me, and Liza started kissing me. Beth massaged my back. It took thirty seconds before I became rock-hard. And all of a sudden both girls went to work on me. We went down in the first inning and didn't come up until the ninth. I never dreamed that anything this incredible could happen. Then they started in on each other. I heard my wife moaning to Beth: oh, yes, yes, yes, yes do that to me . . . They were having a boiling hot time turning each other on. Well, it didn't turn me on. It bothered the hell out of me. We talked it over later and decided that we were going to limit our fantasies to the two of us.

If you're going to make a fantasy come true, not only is trust essential, but you *both* must be interested in doing it and you must be aware that sometimes the results aren't what you might have anticipated. Although Stan's fantasy of a three-way evolved into reality, the effect was a highly negative one. What might have developed into a threatening or highly explosive situation was defused because he and his wife could talk things over freely and agree that the experience was not one they wished to repeat.

There's a new, intrinsically eighties' aspect to the world of sexual fantasy, and most of it has to do with technological advances. All sorts of photographic and electronic equipment have gone sexual. You can fantasize while you watch steamy movies on cable. You can rent or buy what used to be called skin-flicks in your local video shop. You can have germ-free, risk-free fantasy sex via telephone. You can make tapes of yourselves in bed and swap them with willing counterparts. (One entrepreneur in Southern California has set up a thriving tape-swap business and will trade tapes for couples as long as they don't live in the same zip code area.)

You can initiate a smoldering romance via your living-room computer or exchange fantasies at the touch of a keystroke. Although a few therapists regard these new phenomena as alienating and antithetical to intimate relationships, a great many feel they can help to loosen up inhibitions, fire up fantasies, and even make for more intimacy. *Time* Magazine (May 14, 1984) reports that couples who have connected through home computers have "traded phone numbers, photographs and, on at least five occasions, wedding bands."

"We do sex tapes," explains a Los Angeles woman I interviewed. "We bought a VCR and a video camera and then we started taping ourselves making love. As we got more into it, we started doing crazy things we'd never done before. Now we've graduated into making movies. The lighting was the hardest part. We've spent a lot of time perfecting indoor and outdoor shots. Now we're getting costumes, writing scripts, working out sequences—and we stay within the budget we set! It's been a complete turnaround for our love life, and we get a huge kick out of sharing a very special hobby."

Grown-up Toys

Several years ago, when I wrote an article on shops that sold sex aids, the typical establishment had advanced from stereotypically sleazy to fairly straightforward vending of all sorts of articles. Today's shops often call themselves boutiques, and are such an accepted part of the merchandising establishment that they have slick windows featuring stylish mannequins and sophisticated lighting techniques. The merchandise that I saw in one Greenwich Village sex-aid shop last week consisted of the mini-est bikini bathing suits for both men and women. The week before it was underwear à la Calvin Klein.

The black leather masks and chains and whips were still there, but they were way in the back, some under a thin coating of New York grime. A dazzlingly comprehensive assortment of vibrators and cock rings were, to be sure, on display, as were ben-wah balls and latex underpants (which somehow looked unerotically hi-tech to me), but the fastest-moving stuff seemed to be the line in silk jockstraps; men's-style underwear for women; and sexy, lacy, cutout lingerie that one associates with the legendary Frederick's of Hollywood.

Today, books, movies, videos, body lotions, and silk scarves (to be used for "soft, elegant bondage" as one proprietor explained) all qualify as aids in the quest for the enhanced sexual experience. Men used to be the overwhelming majority of customers, but according to an informal survey I did in New York and Los Angeles, there's been a significant increase in women patrons.

Checking out a sex shop has become a pretty safe experience. The sheen of the forbidden is gone and I, for one, lament its passing. However, it does mean that you can go into one of these places without feeling uncomfortable, and if you've never tried a sex aid, you might consider one—or some—if only for the fun of trying out something new. Sex is meant to be playful, and these merchants aim to accommodate with a bounty of toys.

If you can't bring yourself to pass through the door and you're still curious, you can always write away for a catalogue. You'll be surprised at the attractive graphics and tasteful presentation of the merchandise in a variety of mail-order catalogues that regularly advertise in the back pages of respectable magazines like *Ms.* and *Playboy*.

One popular aid that you may not find in a sex shop but may be located in your local drug or housewares store is an electric massager that is usually shaped like a man's rectangular hairbrush. Instead of bristles it has rows of vibrating bands plus one or two straps that fit over the back of the hand. Several men and women mentioned that this was the one mechanical device (besides a vibrator) that was well worth buying. "It's not necessarily for making love," explained a long-time devotee. "We use it to give each other all-over body massages to relax and unwind. It's much easier than giving a Swedish-type massage and takes almost no effort. We feel the best time is after a long tub-soak. When we do use it during sex, we start out massaging and move onto the genitals only when we're really aroused. You have to be very turned on to use it because it might feel like more than you can take, but when you do use it the sensations are incredible!" The manufacturer mentioned most often was Wahl-Clipper, one of whose models comes with two speeds and has an additional contoured heat surface to speed relaxation and give hotly sensuous strokings.

CHAPTER **19**

The Night of Endless Pleasure

ALMOST EVERY MORNING at around eight thirty I head two blocks downtown to the Cupping Room Cafe, where I have a second cup of coffee, read the paper, conduct interviews and/or pore over the words that I've processed the day before.

One day in April, when the World Trade Towers were shimmering in the early spring sun, I ran into a friend of mine who had just put his five-year-old daughter on the school bus and was heading in the same direction down Broadway.

"I'll treat you to some coffee, David," I said, "if you'll talk to me about sex."

"Who could resist such an offer?" He grinned. "You know I've always wanted to be included in your research. And anyway I can't solve a problem in a painting I've been working on so I've got plenty of time to talk."

David is the essence of the new man, a nurturing father who shares equally in his daughter's upbringing, a supportive husband who genuinely cheers on his wife's career, a man who does the dishes—without being asked—a humanist who deeply believes in the women's movement. And he's *very* sexy to boot. His wife, Betsy, has just as much going for her as he does. I've known them for six of the seven years they've been married.

We reached the cafe, ordered coffee and homemade walnut muffins, and began to talk.

"Good sex," he said in answer to my opening question, "is self-affirming. It's something you're comfortable with, makes you feel good. But great sex is an event that pushes your boundaries outward. You're breaking through to something new with the other person. It's a discovery, a surprise—a new state of consciousness. It's an even greater intimacy than you had before."

"Do you mean that good sex is mostly physical and great sex is more in the brain?" I asked.

"That would sum it up," he said.

"Not everyone would agree with your definitions.

But, more importantly, how and when do you have great sex?"

"I think it's easy to have great sex in the first stages of an affair," he said. "But is it possible to have great sex—to feel that kind of exhilaration—*on an ongoing basis*? Is it possible to keep discovering something new about someone who is as familiar to you as your wife?"

He drained his coffee cup, gave me a mischievous smile, and asked, "What have *you* found in your research?"

When I read over my interview with David, I realized that he had hit upon a crucial sexual concern. Wives and husbands, or long-time lovers, are familiar, known quantities. You see them every day. You know how they brush their teeth, you can name the vitamins they take and the ice cream they favor, in short, they don't have the luster they had when new. How then do you avoid the twin devils of *boredom* and *monotony?*

Monotony, Monotony, Monotony

She tosses the strand of minted dental floss into the wicker wastebasket, brushes her teeth, and then *very* gently applies cream around her eyes.

She has three beautiful nightgowns folded in her top drawer: one that she wore on her honeymoon and two that John has given her. She reaches for the white, extra-long T-shirt that she's taken to wearing to bed since Stacy was born. She keeps meaning to wear one of the slinky ones as a surprise to John, but somehow she's never gotten around to it.

John is switching from channel to channel via the remote. "Nothing worth staying up for," he says as she tucks into bed with her book. He turns off the TV. She shuts her book, clicks off the light. They settle down. She arranges her body to fit into his. His arm is thrown over her shoulder, but in a moment he moves and she feels his hand on her thigh, under the T-shirt.

"Just let me go to the bathroom and put in my diaphragm," she says, slipping out of bed. In three minutes she's back. She reaches into the night-table drawer for the body lotion. Squeezing a few drops from the bottle, she begins to rub it on his penis. In a few moments she is lying on her back—T-shirt accordion-pleated on her chest—and he is entering her.

When it's over for him he continues to stroke her until he hears, "Ooh, I'm coming . . ."

Two nights a week—unless work pressures are just too intense—and usually on Sunday morning while the kids are watching cartoons, John and Mary Beth make love. John comes first, and then Mary Beth. Sometimes she doesn't come, but neither one considers it a disaster. Once or twice a month Mary Beth gives John oral sex. Every so often they do it doggy-style (which Mary Beth likes), but the rest of the time it's strictly missionary position. The whole business from John's hand-on-breast to Mary Beth's "Ooh, I'm coming" takes from eight to twelve minutes—including the insertion of her diaphragm.

Scenes like this, or variations thereof, are played out in bedrooms all across this country. Does sex that was once great—as Mary Beth and John say it was for them—have to degenerate into a monotonous, repetitious, predictable routine? How do couples keep it on the edge? Is it possible to sustain a delicious sexual simmer over the long haul?

"It's so easy to let just about anything come before sex—the kids, the dishes, calls to your mother, paying the bills. But if you don't put sex high on your list of priorities, you're going to end up with a low-quality relationship," comments an incredibly busy district attorney whose sixteen-year marriage is enviably intact. She literally blocks out prime time for sex on her calendar!

A psychotherapist in New York who has a wonderfully romantic, strongly sexual bond with her husband, says emphatically, "If you set out to maintain quality sex—to beat boredom and break monotony—it's not so difficult to succeed."

What does it take?

Here's what the experts in the field—researchers, psychologists, and couples who have maintained a sexual high—say is necessary.

"Make sex a priority in your life," say those who keep the sexual fires burning. If you want sex to stay sexy, you have to make it an important part of your life—even if you have to give something up, as a married-just-over-a-year journalist from Nashville, Tennessee, discovered.

"Reading is a passion for me," she explains. "Before I was married my favorite time was when I got into bed with Henry James. My idea of a great vacation was a suitcase full of books and endless time to read. Tom and I have crazy schedules and highly demanding jobs and private time for us is at a premium. Basically I've traded off a lot of my reading for being with him. Making love is very important to us and our sex life would go down the drain if we didn't relinquish some other activity to make time for it."

"Just because you're sweet and good doesn't mean you're physically attractive," says a New York copywriter who emphasizes how easy it is to rationalize slipping out of sexual shape. "It's a myth to think that someone who's let himself go to pot is having great sex."

One therapist I interviewed videotapes his patients during sessions in his office so that they can see how they actually appear to other people. "The surprising thing" he points out, "is that most people look at themselves and say, 'Hey, I'm not that bad.'"

If you've added too many pounds, or overlook such important details as grooming, he suggests that you ask yourself whether you are deliberately trying to appear unattractive to your husband/wife. Do you *want* to turn him/her off? What's the underlying reason for not paying attention to yourself?

Changing your "sexual plan" is another valuable suggestion from sex therapists—a good idea for Mary Beth and John. They make love twice a week: he initiates, she responds. He has an orgasm, then gives her one. They kiss and roll over to sleep.

Most therapists would advise them to break their "script rigidity." Why not have her come first some of the time? Why not turn on the stereo, light some candles, try on a different nightgown, a different cologne, get into bed nude, try a new body lotion or massage oil, set out a glass of wine, a cup of hot chocolate to share after you make love? The idea is very simple: *Change* your established pattern of doing things.

I like this story that a man in Philadelphia told me: "You know that this town has a reputation for being very uptight. I'm married to a woman from the Main Line, which means her background is more straitlaced than most. One night I decided to shake things up a bit. I waited until she was in bed, then got in next to her and put her hand on my crotch. We both sleep nude, but what she felt was not what she expected. She sat straight up like a jackknife and turned on the light. I had on a black jockstrap. She loved it!"

Doing the unexpected keeps romance alive and goes a long way in giving sex an edge. Small, thoughtful gifts—a book of love poems, a bottle of wine from the year you first met—are ways of saying, "I love you and want you."

Nancy, a Boston stockbroker who knows what ticks

sexually and romantically, described how she surprised her husband, Stewart. Stewart had just bought
a new car. In the glove compartment he found a road-
map of Massachusetts with a small town marked by a
big X in red Magic Marker.

"Do you know what this means?" he asked.

"Drive me there this weekend and you'll see," she
replied mysteriously.

When they reached the spot marked X, she instructed him to take a left and then a right.

"Stop here," she announced when they came to a
charming country inn. They were greeted at the desk
by name, and a bottle of chilled wine was waiting
when they entered their room.

"It took quite a bit of planning," admits Nancy, "but
the look on his face was worth it all."

Going to new places is an old idea, but it's still one
of the best ways to keep sex going strong. "People
often protest that a hotel or motel costs too much,"
observes a pastoral counselor in Stamford, Connecticut, "but I'm convinced that a night in new surround-
ings is an inexpensive way to save a marriage."

"New situations allow new possibilities," says an art
director who loves making love in new places. "A different environment frees you to try new things. A
deep armchair placed in front of a mirror, a different
bed and bathroom, another shape of bathtub or
shower stall—they all represent interesting new sexual possibilities."

"I think one of the main reasons relationships fall

apart sexually is that couples tend to spend less time with each other the longer they are together," says a contractor who has vowed to make his second marriage last forever. "When a couple is courting," he continues, "they make time for each other, no matter how busy they are. My wife and I make dates with each other. It worked before we were married and it works now. We have something to look forward to. We take turns making the arrangements and surprising each other."

Here are three stimulating, easy-to-do ideas that come from interviews with men and women who are sensual, creative, and, I suspect, never boring—or bored—in bed.

"Sex means being in touch with your body," says a physiotherapist who works in a New York hospital, "so I like to keep my lover highly sensitized. One evening I was folding the laundry and I had an interesting thought. Later that night we had some great sex and were ready for more. I went into the bathroom and dipped three towels into steaming hot water. Then I squeezed out the water and rolled them into a large version of the little cloths you get in a Japanese restaurant to clean off your hands. I started with her neck and shoulders and then patted and rubbed her entire body. Afterwards she did the same thing for me. It was a fantastic sensation, expecially when she came to my penis." One caution here: When you come to the genital area, wait until the towels have cooled or use lukewarm water.

"I like perfume," says a sophisticated Chicago woman who owns her own retailing business, "and I find that men like it too—especially when it's delivered in ways they don't expect. One night I put four different kinds of perfume on, each in a different part of my body. I told my lover to see if he could name the various fragrances. He told me he had some exotic travels that night. But what really knocked me out was what happened the next night: he came to bed with *my* favorite perfume all over *his* body. 'You like it so much,' he said, 'you should know how wonderful it smells to me.' There was something so deeply sexual about that gesture . . ."

A graduate student from Ann Arbor, Michigan, had this stimulating idea: "My lover and I are always trying new things out on each other. He's brought home erotic books and read them to me, we've explored a lot of the stuff in sex catalogues, but one of the simplest things I ever did was one of the best. We were making love one night and I said to him, 'Listen to this!' I put on a tape of two people making love. All we could hear was the sounds—and they were hot! When he realized it was *us* making love—I had made the tape without his knowing it a few nights before— he was as turned on as I'd ever seen him. We had a wild time that night. We're going to rent a video camera and try that next!"

The Genderless Geisha

As I was doing the research for this chapter, a wise friend gave me a book entitled *Geisha*. (Liza C. Dalby,

University of California Press, 1983) As I read it I realized that the Japanese have one of the most interesting solutions to the persistent problem of sexual ennui: geisha.

Americans may be appalled at the very idea of the geisha. We often picture her as a servile woman who sits behind a man and pours his rice wine and bestows other services as well. Please eradicate everything you've ever known or imagined about geisha. Because buried beneath all our stereotyped notions are some valuable ideas that post-lib American women—*and men*—can find wonderfully useful in beating boredom.

By definition a geisha is a woman, and I'll be using the pronoun "she" in giving the following information, but "he" is equally applicable in most instances. The point I'm trying to make is that the arts of a geisha need not (indeed, should not) be practiced by women only . . .

Here's some background on geisha: A geisha is everything a wife is not. Whereas a Japanese wife is traditionally modest, retiring, devoted to home and family, a geisha is

> entertaining
> flirtatious
> witty
> artful
> alluring
> charming
> skillful
> erotic.

The geisha's principal occupation is to entertain men. The word geisha derives from the word gei, meaning art. Thus a geisha is trained in one or more of the traditional Japanese arts—music, dancing, singing. Her aim is to entertain, to make her clients comfortable, to draw out a shy guest, to engage him in conversation, to make him relax. She draws on a wide repertoire of wit, humor, interest in the contemporary scene, and a highly refined sensitivity to the person she's with.

On a more superficial level, each physical detail is carefully planned. From the magnificent kimono, the design of which makes her walk in a sensuous way, to the perfection of her hair and makeup, a geisha, although she may not be beautiful (and many of them aren't), strives to make herself as attractive as possible.

Sex interestingly enough, in the traditional geisha world, is *not* usually part of the picture. Prostitutes or bar hostesses are available for pure sex. There are certain lower echelons of geisha who "tumble," but they are looked upon with disdain by their classier sisters. Other geisha have long-time patrons where sex is included, but this is a special kind of relationship.

In sum: The geisha is graceful and charming and attentive, her conversation is lively, her silences well-chosen, her toilette is impeccable, her sense of seductiveness highly honed—she makes herself constantly desirable. Her appeal lies *not in novelty* but in her skills at creating an atmosphere of sensuality and sexuality.

However, underlying all the geisha's art is one simple principle of equality: *The true geisha gives only as good as she gets.* Thus a man's response to a geisha's scenario is critical. If she pours *sake* for him, he in turn is expected to fill her cup when it's empty. If she's witty and initiates a conversation, he's expected to contribute, too—and definitely not just in a cursory way. In an evening with a geisha, *both* sexes interact in the kind of richly sensuous and cerebral play that can be a prelude to great sex, and it is men and women who understand these age-old arts of allure and seduction who can have nights of endless pleasure.

CHAPTER 20

Love-Drugs

YES, THERE IS ONE true turn-on substance—the male hormone testosterone. When given to women (for the treatment of certain cancers) it is a powerful sexual stimulant with equally powerful negative effects (hair growth on the chest, voice-deepening, increased levels of aggression). When given to men it usually has no effect sexually.

As of this writing, however, a tree extract has been found to be extremely effective in inducing intense sexual arousal and performance in laboratory animals. Reports of the marvelous aphrodisiacal properties of yohimbine hydrochloride (produced from an evergreen tree growing in Cameroon, West Africa) have been heard of since the 1920s, but were dismissed by most researchers. Today's researchers feel differently. Yohimbine "may be a true aphrodisiac" according to Dr. Julian M. Davidson, a professor of physiology at Stanford University's medical school, where experiments on human volunteers are now being conducted. (Interview, the *New York Times*, August 31, 1984)

We'll have to wait a while to find out how humans react to this fabulous substance, but in the meantime what about drugs that are available? How effective are they?

Opium has been used in India to prolong an erection, but recent researchers have reported the opposite effect. *Cocaine* has been touted as a chic sexual stimulant, but the data are totally inconclusive and there have been contradictory reports. Some of the trendier sexual turn-ons that I heard about include dipping a cotton-tipped swab into cocaine and dabbing it on the rim of the anus and/or vagina. "Cocaine can be used as a local anesthetic," remarks a skeptical physician, "and this practice might numb the sensitized areas, making them susceptible to unintentional harm."

Marijuana is also in scientific limbo in terms of being a turn-on. Some people claim fantastic sexual experiences, but respectable research is still inconclusive. *Amyl nitrite,* a drug used to treat chest pain due to coronary disease, has often been reported as intensifying orgasm, but no carefully controlled studies of its effect—or its safety—have been done as of this writing.

Alcohol may initially serve to lower your inhibitions, but taken in more than moderate quantity it's counterproductive: erections can be easily lost or they don't happen at all.

Blistex, a lip balm that comes in a small tube or in stick form (available at any drugstore), is said to give a heightened sensation when lightly rubbed on nipples, the tip of the penis, or the clitoris. "Dangerous no, pleasurable perhaps," is how one doctor described its effects. Blistex is mentholated, as are some of the lubricants (Hot Lube is a popular one) sold in sex shops. The "kick" comes from the fact that the menthol contributes to the enlargement of minute blood vessels in the skin and thus results in increased sensitivity.

But the best stimulants are both legal and free. They are *love* and *desire.* Is there anything more bewitching than feeling truly loved and truly desired? Simone de Beauvoir (in an interview with Alice Schwarzer, *Ms.* August 1983) said it in her own straightforward way: "I never felt desire for a man if I wasn't desired myself."

Turn-offs

While the search for the great turn-on continues, a very different drug-related aspect has been largely overlooked. This is the fact that many drugs inhibit or impair sexual response. The chemistry and anatomy of arousal is still not fully understood, and labels on both prescription and nonprescription drugs have largely ignored possible sexual side effects. These effects can range from impotence to inhibiting orgasm. If you're taking any drug, *ask* your physician to explain how it relates to your sex drive and your capacity for sexual arousal. You may be taking something that is affecting you in a subtle but significant way.

You can find a comprehensive list of drugs and their possible sexual side effects in Helen Singer Kaplan's outstanding and definitive book, *Disorders of Sexual Desire, Volume II,* published by Simon and Schuster.

CHAPTER **21**

Secrets of a Truly Seductive Woman

ALICE WAS WRITING an article on happily married couples and had made a date to interview Diana over lunch.

"Just start from the beginning and tell me why you think it works so well with you and Michael," she said, clicking on her tape recorder.

"Well," said Diana, leaning back, "Michael has always set challenges for me . . .

"We had been living together for ten months when he said, 'It's Leap Year and you're supposed to do something about it.'

"I thought and thought and nothing wonderful came to mind, but the next day, on my way home, I passed a balloon shop and I knew I had the answer.

"The next morning, Michael's secretary handed him an enormous box. He opened it and dozens of colored balloons with I LOVE YOU written on them hit the ceiling. Twelve architects, eight draftsmen, and six secretaries ran in to see conservative Mr. Boeting's reaction. He loved it!"

"I remember that," Alice said. "He told Jim he thought he would marry you after that one! But go on—"

"A few weeks later," Diana continued, "it was the first anniversary of the famous week we spent in Europe together. This time I said to him, 'You're supposed to do something about it.' That night as we were dressing to go out he brought me a drink.

"I swirled the ice around with my finger so that it would dilute the bourbon. Something caught my eye in one of the cubes. I fished it out and frozen inside was an antique diamond ring!"

Diana spread her fingers slightly and admired, for the millionth time, the lovely round diamond flanked by two small, sparkling sapphires.

"That was eleven years ago!" she said, enjoying her own tale.

Alice checked her tape recorder and said, "Go on. I love hearing this!"

"I still can't believe that man. He's a true romantic. But there's another side to him that took me a while to understand. He needs a great deal of what he calls space. He gets edgy when he doesn't have extended time for himself.

"The occasional night that he spends in his studio is possible only because there's so much trust between us. He's refreshed and happy when he comes back. It would never have worked if I'd clung on to him and said, 'What do you mean you're staying out late tonight?'

"You remember what happened after Dan was born?" Diana asked.

"Of course I do. Jim and I thought it was strange at first and then we realized that he needed to do it. But say it in your own words. I want a lot of direct quotations."

"Okay—I'll just keep talking as if you don't know anything. It's easier to keep things straight, although I don't know how much use this is going to be to you—"

"Di, don't worry. People are dying to know what makes a good marriage tick. Keep talking!"

"I really loved being pregnant. Michael went to all my gynecologist's appointments and Lamaze classes. He liked the way my body was changing—and he was exceedingly moved when Dan was born. But I could see he was strained and needed to get away. He'd made plans to go to an important business meeting in Frankfurt and then canceled because he felt he should stay home with me and the baby.

"I could feel his tension and I said to him, 'Why don't you go to the conference. My mother is terrific with babies. Alice and Jim will keep me company. I'll be fine.' And, as you so well remember, he went. Two days later he called to say he was coming home. I said to him—and I meant it—'Are you sure you want to come back so soon? We're doing fine.' He was home on the next plane. What he really needs is to know that he can have the space if he wants it.

"We talk a lot. When I'm the one who's feeling needy, I tell him right away. If we're in conflict I never let it go too far. We talk about it as soon as possible. Remember after Jessica was born and I got promoted to vice president? I was a wreck and needed to go to a spa and clear my head. It was a particularly bad time for him at his own office, but he told me, 'Go ahead. Don't worry about anything. I'll take care of the kids.'

"So, having our needs filled is a two-way street. That's why it works so well for us.

"There was one important decision I made early on in our relationship. Even though the children are immensely important to us, I was not going to let my relationship with Michael slip. I went to work to get my body back in shape— But I'm getting off the track. What was I saying?"

"You were talking about not letting the kids interfere with your relationship—"

"Oh, yes . . . When we were first married we'd rent a little gray-shingled house in Maine for a whole month. The only things we could see were the moody gray Atlantic and swaying white lobster boats We'd spend tons of time in bed together. Those months in Maine in that cozy cottage always reminded me of the first weekend in Paris where it seemed there was nothing else in the world but the two of us.

"Although the prolonged intimacy we had before they were born is almost impossible now, we make sure we still get it in small doses. We have wonderful times with the kids, but when they're in bed we concentrate on ourselves.

"We keep a lot of evenings free just to be alone. You know, someone once asked what kept us together, and Michael said, 'Sex!' They didn't believe him, but in the largest sense it's true."

Alice nodded and checked her tape recorder once more.

"I think the important thing about sex is to not get into a rut," Diana continued. "I try not to do predictable things, and I never forget the triggers that turn him on. Even though we've been together for over a decade, I try to do something new, something a little surprising. Sometimes we enjoy being silly. Sex is not so serious. But it's incandescent and passionate and it can still shake me to the depths of my soul."

Diana paused, thinking about what she'd said. It was true: she and Michael made love often, they still shared—and cultivated—the intense physical connection that they'd discovered together early in their relationship. Sex was a habit they'd gotten into from that first afternoon in Paris, and it was a habit they never wanted to change.

"When we only had Dan we made love a lot in the morning," Diana continued. "Now that we have the two children I've had to train myself to live on less sleep so we can still have that time together.

"It's a very intense relationship, very trusting and loving. We both work on it. It's naive to think that you don't have to work on a relationship. You do if it's going to last."

Diana stopped suddenly and looked at her watch.

"Alice! I've been talking for an hour. I've got to get back to the office in fifteen minutes. We've got a department meeting scheduled for two thirty. Did you get *any* usable material at all?"

"I can use every last word," Alice assured her. "Is there anything you want to add?"

Diana hesitated, her gray eyes suddenly serious.

"Yes, there is one thing more," she said, "but I don't know whether you'll be able to use it. It happened just last week. I was to meet Michael in front of the Plaza Hotel after work so we could go to a cocktail party together. I was a few minutes early, and I was kind of sauntering over to the hotel entrance when I saw a tall, fair-haired man in a meticulously tailored tan suit. He was just standing there, but he radiated a kind of animal sexuality. I thought to myself, Now, that's an incredibly attractive guy!

"I walked a few steps closer and realized it was Michael! We never did make it to the party."